time to change ...

Before we start
Think about your life. What do you
want to change? What do you want
more of? What would you like to
be better at? Write it all down here,
however big or small. It will help
to focus your thoughts later on …

Home

t do you want to change?

Friendships

....
....
....
....
....
....
....
....
....
....

Fun

....
....
....
....
....
....
....

So … wha

Contents

Part A

How it works

Part B

The instructions

Part C

The tool kit

Family

Job

Wealth

Use this chart to write down anything you want to go for in your life. It can be big or small, easy or tricky. Get it down here and add to it as we go along …

M

What I want to create in my life ...

What I don't want …

Adventure

....
....
....
....
....
....
....
....
....

Love

....
....
....
....
....
....
....

Health

....
....

How it works

In Part A, you will find the foundation principles of how we create our experiences through mind activity. These principles have been spoken about in whispers for generations and across cultures. Once you know how these work, you will be able to start unlocking the power potential of your mind so effectively that you will learn how to bring about any outcome you choose in your life. The principles and the "how it works" of creating a happy life are outlined here and given in an easy-to-understand style.

Part

A

Attract

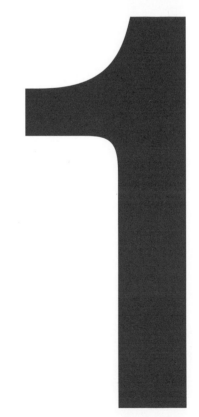

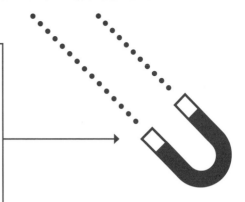

The whole universe is made up of energy.

You are a vibrating magnet.
Your mind is a powerhouse and has a strong attraction-based engine; it attracts things to it that correspond precisely to the thoughts and feelings that are given out. With your mind, you are the most attractive thing in the universe.

We live in an attraction-based world, and we create and pull toward us everything that we experience in our lives. Everything that shows up comes directly from the nature of our thoughts, emotions, and words.

This happens every time, without exception. We are responsible for everything that happens in life, and once we know how this works, we can ride that wave and make it work for us. We can have more love,

better health, more wealth, and more happiness simply by making a few adjustments to the things that we do with our minds.

Sound interesting? Would you like to change your life for the better and get happier right away?

If so, read on.

A. How it works
First off, let's consider the nature of the universe, starting off huge and then ending up small.

Scientists have recently found that the whole universe is *energy-based*. All forms of matter, whether solid, gas, or liquid, are made up of energy. We now understand that, at the atomic and subatomic level, all

Notes:
....
....
....

> **Energy attracts energy of a similar quality and vibration. This is what the Law of Attraction is all about and it works through the laws of physics.**

things can be broken down into smaller and smaller components, which all end up being a form of the same kind of energy.

Human beings are energy. A table is energy. A plant is energy. The sea is energy. Air is energy. Thoughts are energy. Everything is made up of the same stuff and is connected within the same energy matrix. In other words, and in terms of quantum physics, everything in this universe is made of the same stuff. The implications of this are incredibly exciting and as vast as the universe.

To continue with this idea, things which "feel solid" and things that are "fluid" are actually the same; they are simply energy vibrating at certain rates. We are all operating within the same huge energy field. We truly are "all one" and from the same big clump of energy. You and I are the same; we are energy beings. Where we live is an energy universe. We come from the same material and same energy mass—it's all one great big universal energy system that we are swaying and whooshing about in right now.

This universal energy is intelligent and creative and it transmutes into things straight from its original form.

How does it do this? It starts with thoughts.

> **Everything is made of the same creative stuff—the putty of life is all the same.**

Because everything is of the same stuff, there is a correspondence between all things—everything is connected to everything else at some level. This has enormous consequences in the field of mind, physics and life-change. **Energy vibrates at different rates and has different qualities at these different rates or "frequencies."**

Matter is quite dense and compact and, therefore, is slow to move or change. For example, a rock face, being very dense, would be slow to change but, over time, it would gradually erode. Water changes much more easily and is affected by external temperature and forces quite quickly. Thoughts are a much lighter form of energy than either of these, and are capable of changing swiftly and easily—in a moment.

B. Energy is magnetic
How does this idea relate to our thoughts, feelings, and visualizations? As these are all energy-based forms,

Notes:
....
....
....

((•)) Vibrate

Attract

they attract life experiences which mirror and reflect the content of our thoughts and feelings back to us.

Now we know and understand that how we think and feel magnetically attracts what comes to us in our lives. Once we become aware of this scientific fact, we can see why thinking positively is so important to having a happy life, as it directly affects and creates the positive things that show up in our lives. It now becomes really clear how important it is to keep a handle on what we feel, think, and talk about and the vibration of the people that we spend our time with.

All of these aspects affect the kind of lives that we have right now. Everything that has shown up in our lives so far is a direct result of our earlier mind activity. This is true for absolutely everything you are experiencing in your life today.

C. I am attracted to you

We live in an attraction-based universe and all things are magnetic. Our life conditions are simply and purely affected by the energy and vibrational mix of the thoughts and feelings emanating from our magnificent minds.

It's important to know that the information given here is scientifically proven. Once you get this, you can really see and appreciate that what we think and feel does affect our futures.

We must be careful and disciplined to think, feel, and sense the things that we choose to bring into our lives. Everything we think about and focus on, we magnetically attract directly into our experience. From this moment on, now that you know this, **you will be more aware and careful about what you think, say, do, feel, imagine, and wish for.**

D. Thoughts become things

A thought is a very light, malleable form of energy. Unlike denser forms of energy, thoughts can instantly start the process of creating an experience. An idea in the mind is always the first component of anything happening in life and it is a thought that precedes our life experiences or "manifestations." In order to plan a vacation, you first have the thought of going on vacation. With the thought in motion, the vibration is set up and sent out like an e-mail that will attract the manifestation of the thought in physical terms—before you know it the

Notes:
....
....
....

Attract

We need to upgrade our
positive thinking,
feelings, and focusing.

thought vibrates back and turns into a physical manifestation in your life.

> **man·i·fest** verb
> *to make evident to the senses, especially to the sight; to show plainly; to reveal or display what may have at first been obscured or hidden; to appear in visible form.*

E. Law of Attraction

What we think about and focus on materializes in our lives. When you are positively thinking about good things, you will attract them. Similarly, if someone is focused on doom, gloom, or unhappiness, you don't have to be a genius to work out what they will be actively attracting into their world.

It is simply a law of physics. The physics of waves and particles means that **you will get more of whatever you're thinking most about attracted to you.** The focus point of your attention will be the trigger for what is manifested directly into your world.

We must focus less on the bad news, on the miserable, and on the negative. In order to attract happy lives, we need to concentrate on all good things, filtering out what we have already and focusing on

what we would like to attract. This is assuming we want to create wonderful abundance and harmony in our lives. It is my guess that you may be looking for more good things to come in—rather than doom, gloom, and an increase in unhappiness—if you're reading this book.

Sometimes our negative beliefs and negative programming get in the way of the process of looking on the bright side; however it is necessary to stamp out these beliefs in order to be able to think positively and focus on what you want. (We will show you how to sort this out later in the book.)

Sure enough, what you are expecting will show up; whatever you believe will come into play. Does this sound familiar to you? This explains why, when life gets better, it just keeps getting better, and when you feel that you can only attract bad stuff, you attract more bad stuff and head off in a downward direction generally, confirming your beliefs.

It's all about your mind-set. We need to change your mind-set from one of lack to one of abundance and then watch life catch up with this belief. Go there first with your mind-set, and let life follow.

Notes:
....
....
....

F. You create your reality

Just thinking positively won't crack the nut. There is more to it than this. The good news is that it's very simple once you know how, and it all gets explained in this book.

We carry blocks deep inside that we are not even aware of and that hold us back. Once we see these and release them, we are on our way, and these old blocks are doomed. We can move forward without being stuck.

There are powerful methods which will help us to identify these old patterns and beliefs that are hurting us. Once we have identified them we can then use mind power techniques to kick these beliefs out of our lives forever. Belief-busting techniques for doing this easily and powerfully are given in Part C.

As you go through and get to understand this area of creating your life by design, take note of any obstacles or recurring negative "mind chatter" that comes up, so that you can identify it and then clear it easily when you get to that point.

Many of us have blocks and mind program patterns that no longer support us. These need to be cleared out and replaced with more positive, abundance-building beliefs.

Make a change

Find a place where you will be fine to relax. Allow yourself to imagine a new experience, set a positive intention, and give thanks that life is changing. Know that great things are already happening to you.

The setup for fast and positive life changes comes in now.

The instruction to your unconscious is to simply and swiftly make the mind changes necessary, adjust to the new downloads, and update your inner operating software.

Audio 01: This audio will give you the tools to begin and get you ready to make some big changes for the better. Audio

---

Notes:

....

....

....

Chapter 1 checklist	☑
Your mind is like a magnet	☐
Everything is made up of energy and all energy is magnetic	☐
Thoughts and feelings attract corresponding experiences	☐
We become what we think and feel	☐
We create our realities with our thoughts and emotions	☐
Leave negative, toxic, bad news and gossip behind	☐
Focus on the good stuff to have a great life	☐

Notes:

....

....

....

Imagine

12

Playdreaming is great.

Every moment we are awake (and sometimes while we sleep), we are effortlessly visualizing. We are dreaming, imagining, playing out ideas and storylines with our minds and our powerful imaginations.

We imagine, daydream, and visualize nearly all of the time. We take notice of what is going on through some or all of our senses, and this is the way we make sense of our world and what we consider to be reality. This imagination power is an important player in the mechanics of creating your own reality or consciously "manifesting."

How well we play with our internal mind machinery and our imaginations dictates how happy our lives become.

A. Visualization

The technique of visualization (or imagination or hallucination—call it what you will) is the first of the major tools for creating the life you choose. It is a technique that anyone can do easily and effortlessly. It means you use your imagination to create what you want to bring into your experience. This is a natural process for our minds and we use it daily in our normal lives.

We use the power of our minds to think, and make pictures and associations around thoughts. For example, if I ask you to think about or "creatively visualize" your own front door, you would go inside your mind and put up some sort of reference or image relating to what your front door looks like to you. You may see

Notes:
....
....
....

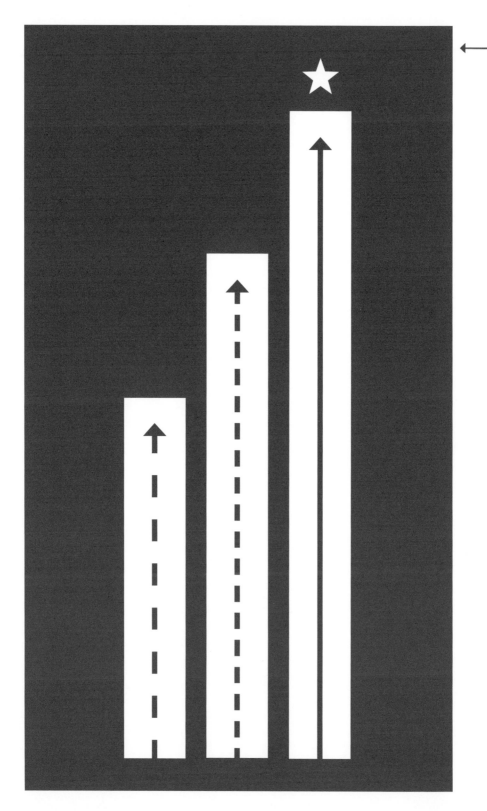

The stronger we feel, the more anything is possible.

the color or the frame and the shape. This may appear as a picture, a feeling, or some kind of "sense" of it. It may be a combination of any of these. Whatever it is and whatever method you used inside your mind, you have creatively visualized your own front door. You have made a visual or mind representation—a creative visualization—of the idea. This is a key component in successful manifesting and creating.

B. Get creative with visualization
Many of us use creative visualization without even realizing it. We do this while asleep and awake; we may visualize getting out of bed or making a drink, taking a shower, or getting dressed, even before we open our eyes in the morning. This chapter will show you how to use imagining as a tool in designing your own life—new

and improved – starting right now.

Images, patterns, sounds, voice tracks, feelings, senses, thoughts, and ideas all flow through our minds. Some of us make pictures, others mind-movies, some use a mixture of ways of doing creative visualization; we all have different ways of dealing with our thinking and coding how we interact with the world around us.

Designing your life for a positive outcome requires you take control of your visualizations. Whatever you think about and focus on is what you are attracting and directly choosing to bring into your life. When your mind wanders around and lands on things that make you feel bad, learn to move your thoughts away, and shift your attention onto something that makes you feel better.

Visualization: "Playdream"

Imagine yourself now being wise, confident, feeling good, and being able to construct the life of your dreams with full-blown optimism. Imagine an impressive voice, inside your mind, saying "*I can sense/see/ feel/imagine how I can do this easily.*"

Audio 02: This audio is designed to make you feel strong, optimistic, and confident.

Audio

Notes:
....
....
....

Get in the flow.

There are different strengths in visualizing. We can visualize in crisp full color, with a strong focus, mixed with powerful feelings, or we may use a foggy and unclear image without color and without a soundtrack which will mean we have less clarity on things. The stronger the image, the stronger the feeling and the more powerful the pull into your life experience.

C. Positive visualization

An important component in the mix of manifesting is being in a peaceful, relaxed state with a positive mental attitude while you are visualizing and imagining your future. We can all remember a time when we felt angry or upset and know that it can be very difficult to concentrate or focus on what we are meant to be doing. Being in a negative mental state immediately sets up barriers to being in the flow or getting things done the way you would like.

Many of us have experienced the feeling of being on top of our game, feeling strong and positive, and then seeing that things work out with a lot less effort when we have this perspective. We have to push less and things just go with the flow. When we are happy, feeling good, loved and supported, it's much easier to feel that anything is possible.

In order to create life experiences positively and easily, it's necessary to be in a positive frame of mind. **This opens up the gates that let you get into the flow and begin powerful manifesting.**

One great technique to achieving a positive mental state is to close your eyes, do some deep breathing, get into a relaxed state and allow yourself to remember a time when you felt happy and positive. It might be a time when you were away on vacation, a time when you were congratulated for an achievement, or a time when you were doing a good job for someone or receiving an acknowledgment for something done well. Pull out a good memory from your memory banks and spin it around inside your mind and through your body.

Float and spin it; feel the feeling; see the picture of it and hear the soundtrack of what it sounds like and spin it all through your body. If you're having trouble pulling up a memory, then make one up. This works just as well and is completely effective. Using all of your senses powers up the effect—get the feeling, the smell,

Notes:

....

....

....

> **Use your imagination—it's like a muscle. The more you use it, the better it gets.**

the touch, the image, the movie, and the sounds of the experience—pull all of this in together and flood your body with it.

D. Real or made up? In reality, it doesn't matter

It is worth emphasizing a very important point here. Your mind cannot tell the difference between a made-up or imagined idea that you visualized and a real one that you have experienced. The brain treats it as true anyway and attracts accordingly. If you think you are rich, your mind will believe you. It will believe whatever you choose to imagine, whether true or made up.

The best time to do your creative visualizations is when you are in a relaxed, comfortable state. The brain wave that you get into just as you are waking up or going to sleep is particularly good for this.

These are the best times to run your imagination on full power for manifesting. As you wake up and just before you go to sleep something magical happens. Our brains are fully primed to receive instructions most readily in our day.

What if I can't?

Occasionally, there are people who believe they cannot visualize. This is usually because of emotional blocks of some sort. They may have an unwillingness to go inside and stir up unwanted emotions that they believe are best left buried deep inside. It may be these people do not want to reach their emotions for fear of what would happen if the floodgates were to open.

Whatever the reasons, know that it is safe to go within and play with your imagination. Your brain is built to be an imagining device. Just notice anything that comes up during the process of visualizing and allow the thoughts to pass through, gently and easily. For the majority of people, visualizing is familiar and straightforward. It comes naturally and easily. **The more consciously you do it, the better you get at manifesting the good stuff.**

E. Imagine what you want to create

Make sure that what you are visualizing represents what you are truly looking to bring into your life. Be careful not to focus on or visualize things you do not want to bring into your life. Always remember that what

Notes:

....

....

....

> **All messages are taken and received as if they are in the positive.**

you put your focus on comes into your experience. This is law.

So, for example, if you feel you do not have enough money in your life right now, would it be sensible to start visualizing and focusing on this lack of money and the fear that goes with it? No.

In manifesting terms, you turn the situation around by focusing on a positive feeling of the very thing you choose to bring in: having an abundance of money in your life. The *"I don't have enough money"* idea is turned around to the *"I already bring plenty of money into my life and I'm feeling good inside"* idea.

It is important to note that the mind sends out same-vibration action messages, and the universal machine always reads these in the positive. It cannot compute a negative—it just isn't the way it works.

For example, *"I don't want debt"* would be received as a sense that *"I am focused on debt. Please activate this idea further for me and show me more debt."* The universal energy, without judging your choice, comes to deliver to you what is apparently being chosen here; therefore, it

produces outcomes which bring more debt experience into your life. This is probably not your desired outcome. Yet, many people spend a lot of their day chewing over the fact that they have debt and not enough money. This approach will simply perpetuate the debt story. Instead of this it's better to focus on an idea such as, *"I choose to have financial abundance now. I have plenty of examples that I am truly wealthy already."* This idea will instantly pivot you and point you towards attracting an abundant result.

> **Other positive focus examples:**
>
> *"I choose to be in a happy relationship."*
>
> *"I'm already in lots of happy relationships."*
>
> *"I love being loved and I already am."*

Then notice all the examples where this is true.

If you put your thoughts into the negative, then your statements and thoughts will keep you in the space of being on your own. *"I don't want to be on my own. I am lonely and I'm fed up with being on my own"* will be read in mind-attraction terms as: *"I am focusing on being on my*

Notes:

....

....

....

Imagine

Frame your ideas
positively, taking away
any negative aspects.

A three-point plan for positive creative visualization

01. Choose the idea you wish to form.

Decide on the topic or theme of your visualizing. This may be a new partner, a new car, a job you love, a slimmer body, or simply to feel happier.

own, I am always on my own. This is what I do (give me more because I am focusing on this)." This will simply result in more of the same. So as you can see, the framing is very important. Choose the positive frame.

The first time you do this, you may want to choose something that is not too far from your grasp currently. It is best to choose something that feels very possible and within reach to begin with. Keep the idea positively linked to what you are choosing to bring forward into your life right now.

You can do this, even though it is the very opposite of what we have been shown to do in life, in many cases. More often than not, we are taught to swap bad news stories, discuss the dramas, and the things that are going wrong. **The question** *"How are you?"* **often activates the** *"let me tell you exactly what is going wrong in my life at the moment"* **story.** This is a habit and one that will lead to bringing in the negative and making your life go downhill fast rather than uphill fast.

02. Create pictures, feelings, sensations, and a soundtrack of the idea in your mind.

Pictures
Gather together in your mind an appropriate positive picture, image, "mind-movie," or sense of the subject so that it creates a strong positive response in you.

So begin by noticing this, start to change it, and make a choice to start spinning things around, going for what is good and holding that focus as steady as possible.

Feelings
Next, add some strong, positive feelings about your idea into the mind mix. For example, if you would like to add the feeling of excitement, then remember what if feels like to be excited and run this memory until you get the feeling moving in your body. Take this feeling, spin it around inside, and then spin it more, and move it up and down in your body until

Hold your thoughts steady with a positive focus on what you want.

Notes:

....

....

....

....

....

....

....

you feel full of that feeling. Keep this feeling of excitement running as you visualize the pictures.

Taste and touch
Add in a sense of taste, touch, and sensation to your imagined idea too, if this aspect is easy for you: add in whichever of the senses help you to get strong feelings and a sense of the idea being "real."

Sounds
Now add a sound track to your visualization. You may imagine a beautiful, gentle sound of the sea or a more vibrant, upbeat sound to accompany the pictures and feelings. Use whatever works for you, gets you feeling great, and makes the feeling stronger. Listen to an inner soundtrack that makes you feel really good.

Mix it all together
The pictures, feelings, tastes, touch, and sound sensations will work together to give you a strong sense of enjoying the thing you are manifesting, and then hold the feeling, as long as possible, of being the person who already has this aspect showing up in life.

A quantum physicist explained to me that in his cutting-edge lab work on mind change it is this aspect of combining the effect of all of the senses that really connects the dots to power up the method of creating. It works best with details, feelings, and putting yourself inside the picture, as if you are actively participating in it in real time. You are observing you in the picture in your mind's eye. The observational aspect of manifesting is a trigger for success—we will find out why as we go along.

03. Give the idea focus and thanks.

Focus on this visualization for one to two minutes at least five to ten times a day. Twenty times a day is even more powerful. You get the picture.

Bring your idea into focus in your mind as often as you can. The more you do it, the stronger the effect will be. Integrate it into your thinking, allow yourself to believe it's already real, and be aware of yourself feeling good about it. Focus and focus again, clearly and gently.

Give love to the image and warm positive feelings to go alongside the visuals. The feeling is an important component of the triggering process. You can add to this mix some positive statements or affirmations which will help kill any negative mind chatter in that moment.

Add in some gratitude for already having this, and let yourself know that you are allowing this in right now.

You do not need to "push" or try too hard. Gently is the way to go.

F. Karma

This is powerful stuff. Be aware that creative visualization will only work well for positive intentions. You cannot hope to use this for bad or to cause others to suffer without getting hold of the negative aspects and suffering yourself. If you use creative visualization with bad intent, you simply trigger the laws of karma, which means that your intention will come spinning back to *you*. It happens this way because of the magnetic pull of intentions.

If you are thinking bad thoughts or evil intentions toward another, this energy returns directly to you. What you intend for another person will simply be manifested inside you by the Law of Karma and by the Law of Attraction.

Equally, if you are going around sending out love and good intentions to others, then by the same token equivalent things or better will fly back at you like a boomerang.

What you focus on will show up in our own life. From this, we can see why it is important to maintain feelings of optimism, positivity, and goodness. The more you focus on what you would like to manifest, the more easily this shows up directly in your life.

G. Creative visualization rules

The visualization rules are that the idea must be framed as though happening *in the present time*, as if it is already happening in your life. It must also be visualized in a relaxed and gentle way, without forcing any of these feelings.

If you are being forceful with the idea in your mind, it will have the effect of pushing the idea further away and potentially out of your grasp—the very opposite of what you are setting out to achieve. Be gentle with your focus—light as a feather and softly is the route for success.

All people have their own *free will* and this must be respected. We cannot hope to change others. We can only seek change in ourselves with this work. Often by doing this work on ourselves, we notice incredible changes in how people around us respond, and often we witness extraordinary new behaviors coming from others when we make changes. As we create new experiences in our lives by training our own minds, then the benefits are seen all around us.

Notes:

....

....

....

Chapter 2 checklist	☑
We visualize as part of everyday life	☐
Learn to visualize positively, as this shapes your experiences	☐
Visualize in a peaceful, relaxed state	☐
Waking up and going to sleep are the strongest times to create	☐
Only use these tools for your *own* life—not the lives of others. Use these tools only for good. Otherwise, negative outcomes will come back to you	☐
Present all ideas in the positive—not the negative	☐
Be gentle with forming ideas—don't force them	☐
Add positive feelings and emotions to your visualizations	☐
Focus on the topic often but without "pushing"	☐
Feel thanks and gratitude for your intentions already being present	☐
Frame your intentions in the present, as if they're already here	☐

Notes:

....

....

....

Affirm

❝

I want . . . :

01. ....
02. ....
03. ....
04. ....
05. ....
06. ....
07. ....
08. ....
09. ....
10. ....

We cannot reach any goals if we don't know what our goals are. This may seem obvious. However, from my work mentoring, I have found that when asked about their goals, over 90% of people cannot clearly define what they truly want in life with clarity. Indeed, many have never considered this question.

What do you want in life? **Take a moment to write down ten things that you would really like to bring into your life right now.** Be specific, be clear, and go wild with the ideas.

Make sure you keep this list positive and specific.

Setting clear intentions is the starting point in creating what you want in life. Without clear goals, you will be floating all over the place without focus or aim.

We each have an internal GPS, a genius tool designed to take us from A to B easily and effortlessly. Our job is to establish our desired destination, but not to state the route of how we get there. This route is often different from what we might expect, and this adds to the fun of life.

A first step on the road to successful manifesting is to define your goals, set some intentions, and to power these up with affirmations visited regularly in your mind.

Know where you are going— it's the only way you can be sure to get there.

Notes:
....
....
....

I would like to create . . .

A. Intentions

Sit down with a piece of paper and write down what you would like to create in the next week, month, six months, year, five years, ten years, and beyond. Write away and do not edit yourself. Give yourself free rein to be creative and aim high with your intentions. Do this process regularly.

. . . in the next week:

. . . in the next month:

. . . in the next six months:

. . . in the next year:

. . . in the next five years:

. . . in the next ten years:

. . . and beyond:

Once you are clear on what you would like to create, you can take some small steps to start heading in the right direction. All good ideas and new openings begin with having the idea, taking a few first steps, and feeling good in the process.

My desires:

_____

_____

_____

_____

_____

_____

_____

_____

_____

_____

_____

_____

Life is about change, so these intentions should change, expand, and develop over time. They won't necessarily stay the same, and this

is the beautiful nature of life. We are setting new desires and intentions all the time. We are never done with building new desires.

af·fir·ma·tion noun
a statement asserting the existence or the truth of something; something declared to be true, a positive statement or judgment.

B. Affirmations

The best way to power up your intentions is through the setting up of specific intention statements or "affirmations." These affirmations are great for adding strength to the mind-creation process.

Affirmations can be used effectively to help design your life. They can also help your brain recognize and compute new ways of thinking about your world—ways in which reality can be more positively framed to help run your life more easily.

Remember that your brain does not know the difference between "real" and "made up"; as far as your mind is concerned, if it has the sense of an idea (by it being imagined), the mind will consider it "real" and bring in experiences to correspond with this.

Notes:
....

....

....

How to structure and use your affirmations

01. Give a clear statement of intention to work alongside your visualization.

02. Turn this statement into the present tense and make it active, as if you are doing it already.

03. Make it personal by including your own name in the statement.

04. Make the affirmation *specific*.

For example, if you were to ask for "*more money*" in your statement construction, then the question remains, "*how much money?*" How is the universe able to supply accurately when this is so open-ended? The universe doesn't judge or augment what you ask for: You simply get exactly and precisely what you are intending. So be specific.

05. State affirmations in the positive and in terms of what you *do* want, rather than what you *don't* want.

As we have learned already, the universe at the most basic level does not "read" the negative aspect; it will take your statement literally and as if it is stated as a positive. If you were to say, "*I don't want to be poor*" or "*I don't want to be alone,*" then the universe will take this instruction as a request for being poor or for being alone, and will correspond by maintaining this reality for you. Instead, reframe it in terms such as "*I already have millions of dollars*" or "*I already have a beautiful, loving relationship in my life.*"

06. Keep the statements simple, clear, and concise.

These may be spoken inside your mind to yourself or out loud, or written down. Some people like to speak them out loud and record them, playing them back regularly. Check the language; you will get precisely what you ask for, so pay attention to the details of what you are asking for.

Top five ...

Now for your top five ...
It is no good just understanding the theory, unless you actually experience it and put it into practice. Let's begin this now. Write five positive statements of intention and shape them into affirmations using the rules explained in this chapter. Begin now.

Take a moment and complete the following carefully . . .

....

....

....

....

....

....

....

....

....

....

....

I give thanks for this—or something better—appearing in my life for the best.

Date ....

Notice how much this directs your thoughts and feelings toward feelings that are better, brighter, and more optimistic.

C. Feelings

01. As you say your affirmations, get the feeling and sense that it has already happened. Be aware of the feeling and the meaning behind your affirmation. **Feel good about it. Breathe it in and "know it." Smile with it.** When the smile comes naturally, you know that you have activated it positively inside, with good feelings.

02. You may successfully use several affirmations at any one time for focus. Keep one idea per affirmation and make each simple and clear.

03. Affirmations may be used on their own or alongside visualizations. Either way, they are life-changing and powerful.

04. The most powerful times for affirmations to take effect are straight after you wake up and just before you sleep.

05. Affirmations are not about changing the past (although this can be done with more advanced manifesting processes). They are about setting up for the present and apparent future aspects of life. Apparent future aspects are being modeled, shaped, and redesigned constantly, according to our mind's activity.

06. Affirmations serve to reset your internal compass direction toward your chosen point. If you are feeling discomfort about where you are now, this will also help give you relief and a sense of re-direction and new focus.

07. Affirmations help to clear up negative self-chatter. While you are telling yourself something positive about a situation and focusing on what you want, opposing or negative aspects cannot access airtime inside your mind. Negative chatter gets dissolved and lost in the mind mix in favor of a more positive focus.

08. The more you tell your mind that you already have the thing of choice, the more you'll believe it is true and the more the universal energy will bring this into your reality. The stronger the focus and belief that it is so, the faster the set up of attraction into your experience.

Notes:

....

....

....

Example affirmations

"I, Homer, already understand what it feels like to live my life calmly, without drama."

"I, Marge, already know what it feels like to be safe."

"I, Bart, already know what it feels like to listen and be heard by others."

"I, Lisa, already have success in my life, day by day."

"I, Maggie, already have the feelings of making good decisions in my life."

After these affirmations, add a line of gratitude, certainty, and witnessing that it is already present:

"Thank you. It's done. Show me."

There are various aspects to consider in wording your chosen intention including:

"I already know …"

"I already know how to …"

"I already know that it is possible for me to …"

"I already have the feelings of …"

"I already have the experience of …"

Affirm

Top five affirmations:

01. ....
....
....
Thank you. It's done. Show me.

02. ....
....
....
Thank you. It's done. Show me.

03. ....
....
....
Thank you. It's done. Show me.

04. ....
....
....
Thank you. It's done. Show me.

05. ....
....
....
Thank you. It is done. Show me.

Signed ....

Note:
Read these affirmations out loud a few times, then repeat them again to yourself quietly.

D. Keep it private

These should be your own statements and not for someone else, nor created by someone else for you. Only you know what you want to choose to bring into your own life for your best and most productive outcome. Be honest about your own choice of affirmations.

You do not need to share this with others; manifesting works best when you keep it private. Do not invite others to comment or critique your statements, unless it's with a personal coach or mentor.

It is not possible to instruct an affirmation to affect another person's life or an outcome for them. We can only attend to our own lives and must accept that others have free will in operation around theirs. All the work we do inside is about ourselves, not others.

If you have resistance or negative feelings rise up to an affirmation you choose, then notice this and note it as an area where you may need to release energy blocks. Your ego may be stopping you from making this change. This is a powerful and significant area where people get tripped up, and you will be given

the tools to deal with this later.

E. Using affirmations

Using affirmations will help change your mind-set to positive, it will clear up fuzzy thinking around your choice points, and it will set your mind in the right direction. This will trigger the manifesting and the magnetic attraction into your life experience.

Affirmations are strong, positive statements that something is already so. They make the ideas which you have been imagining firm, so they direct your inner focus more sharply, making it more deliberate and with greater focus to the direction of your choosing. They are the steps for manifesting the life of your dreams.

At this point, you may well be saying to yourself, *"If only this was all true, my whole life could transform for the better ..."*

Yes, it can. The good news is that this works and the things you are learning here are the keys to making your life magnificent. Just start believing it and begin to see it working in action, and experience the effects showing up in your life with tangible results.

Notes:

....

....

....

Life gets better starting now.

YES!

Chapter 3 checklist	☑
Affirmations are a power tool for manifesting	☐
State intentions and affirmations only in the positive	☐
Keep it simple and clear with one idea only per affirmation	☐
Include your name for best results	☐
Say your affirmations as if they are already showing up in your life	☐
Be specific; for example, state how much money you want	☐
Add feelings, pictures, and tastes for 3-D powering up	☐
Add "Thank you. It's done. Show me." at the end of each one	☐
Write your affirmations, say them, repeat them, and feel that they're already present	☐
First thing in the morning and last thing at night are the best times to practice and repeat affirmations	☐
Say your affirmations inside your mind and out loud	☐
Add affirmations to visualizations	☐
Affirmations boost mind power and clarity	☐

Vibrate

The better we feel, the better life becomes.

A. States affect our vibration

Our states and moods affect our emotions. These, in turn, affect how we filter our own versions of our lives and our personal perception of the world. All of this dictates how we vibrate and, therefore, what we attract toward us.

Like a radio transmitter our rate of vibration corresponds to a broadcast frequency. Say, for example, we are happy—in this case, our rate of vibration corresponds to a broadcast station like "Radio Happiness" on 111 Hz. As we tune in to this frequency, we attract more of the same energy at the same frequency back to us, through the Law of Attraction. This affects how we see things, and alters our perceptions of the world and how

we see "reality." If we are feeling happy, we will be filtering for more of this goodness, and we will be noticing all things that are good in the world and which correspond to our happy vibrations. If we are feeling predominantly negative emotions, such as anger, upset, fear, guilt, or frustration, then we are more likely to notice that bad things start appearing on our radars to make us increasingly more angry, upset, fearful, guilty, or frustrated. We will be noticing the bad things in our lives and filtering for more and more examples to make our current point of view true. This, in turn, will cause us to "see" more negative things, and so it goes . . .

The better we feel, the better our lives become. The worse things appear to us, the worse things will

(((•))) **Vibrate**

Notes:
....
....
....

seem to get. Whatever we believe to be true for us will become so: good, bad, or indifferent.

We can choose and find examples of any of the things we are looking for in life. Usually it is true, that if we look for something, we will find it somehow showing up. Life has a habit of corresponding to our beliefs that way.

For successful manifesting, you need to choose an emotion and a "being state" which is going to get you attracting good things. This is why it's far better to keep reaching for a better feeling state, every time, no matter what baseline state you are starting from.

So we have seen that our "state of being" affects our rate of vibration and this will affect what we attract into our lives. From the perspective of happiness and feeling good, we will be filtering at rates that are attracting our desires easily and effortlessly.

Let us go over this idea again, as it is so important to understand. If we are looking at things negatively, then we will be attracting all things corresponding to these negative vibrations, and so we will be drawing in negative aspects by magnetizing them straight to us. Conversely, happiness, health, and wealth can all be found on the wave band at the high frequencies of the corresponding good moods and feelings.

To get happy, healthy, and wealthy, go there first in your "being" state, stay in **high frequency,** and hang out with people who vibrate this same high frequency too.

My high-frequency friends:

_____

_____

_____

_____

_____

_____

_____

_____

_____

Notes:

....

....

....

B. Slide up the scale

These ideas show us why it is important to be in a state of *feeling good* as much as possible. It may be that you're not feeling good at this current time in your life and you may be thinking, "but how do I get from down here to up there in my feelings? It is so far away; it feels impossible."

The best advice is to choose a better feeling *straightaway*. You can go up the emotional scale, feeling better and better with each step. Do it gradually and step by step, if you find that you can't jump up to a much better feeling in one go.

It is not always easy or possible to make a massive change in state and to go from, for example, feeling despair straight to feeling happiness. The best route is to gradually work through choosing better feeling states, *step by step*, in ways that are manageable and achievable for you.

C. Change your state

We do this all the time. For example, you change from being in a neutral emotion to sad in a moment when you watch a sad scene in a movie. If you see a friend you haven't seen in a while, your face lights up with appreciation and pleasure at seeing them—instant state change. Someone may reach over and kiss you—instant state change. You get a compliment out of the blue—instant state change. You get a call telling you you've been offered the job you were after—instant state change.

Now, just for the purposes of accessing a new, improved feeling, *imagine* any one of those good things happening, and gently take hold of the corresponding new state that comes in, hold it, and align to it. Your brain will not know the difference between an imagined and an actual event for this purpose, so you can get into the desired state just by imagining a more positive scene in your mind.

This will work. Try it now.

My state changers:

_____
_____
_____
_____
_____
_____

Notes:
....
....
....

Station	+ High vibration
Love and bliss	
Joy	
Peace	
Tranquillity	
Enthusiasm	
Happiness	
Eagerness	
Positive expectation	
Optimism	
Hopefulness	
Contentedness	
Playfulness	
Neutral baseline	
Bored	
Pessimistic, frustrated	
Irritated, annoyed	
Overwhelmed	
Disappointed, doubtful	
Worried	
Blaming, discouraged	
Anger, revenge, rage	
Jealous	
Guilty, unworthy	
Fearful	
Grief, despair, hopeless, feeling like it's the end	− Low vibration

Visualization: "Feeling Good"

If you want to choose a better feeling, go up the chart and choose a feeling above where you are now and work your way up steadily. Go to the new emotion first in your mind, imagine feeling it, and then let the rest of you catch up to this new frequency. One approach to do this is to remember a time when you felt better and go into the memory; get a smile and align with the improved feeling you had then. Or *imagine* having a better feeling and tell yourself to go there; actually pull up the desired feeling in your body and in your senses. Your body will take you there if you ask it. Now choose to take on this feeling and align it within your body. Feel like this feeling is now part of you. Notice that you are feeling better; breathe as you do this to help relax yourself and all aspects of your being.

Environment: Taking yourself out of your regular environment will help this process. Go for a walk outside in the air with some grass under your feet; listen to some happy, uplifting music; watch a comedy; watch the world go by and occupy yourself with some new thoughts— fresh and improved. Your feeling and being state will shift by doing this (it has to, by the way).

Audio 03: This audio will change your state and make you feel a whole lot better.

 Audio

Step by step

Many of us have been taught a default position for our feeling states by our families, peer groups, and colleagues. We often match the states of those around us and tend to mirror the vibrations and states of others nearby. This leads the smart thinkers to realize that it is important to filter who you spend your time with. Make good choices and observe how others affect your feeling state. If someone in particular brings you down and makes you feel bad, notice this and be resistant to it with all your might. Make better choices to be around people who make you laugh and feel good.

Notes:

....
....
....

> **Only you are the architect and designer of your feelings inside.**

D. Kickers

There are many things which can speed us into high- or low-frequency states easily. Here are some examples. Begin to notice what affects you in your life and make the necessary adjustments.

High-vibration enhancers:

Meditating, listening to uplifting music, walking in nature, hearty laughing, eating high vibration food (e.g. colorful fresh vegetables and fruit), giving help to others, singing, dancing, moving around, exercise, love.

Low-vibration enhancers:

Drugs, alcohol, cigarettes, toxic gossip, news, newspapers, certain food (e.g. meat, processed foods), sugary drinks or sodas, listening to negative song lyrics, aggression, anger, rotting smells.

It is a good idea to move away from things that make you feel bad and toward things that make you feel good. This includes people, events, places, movies, news, entertainment, and thoughts. All of these aspects need careful consideration, as **you get to decide how you will influence your own state of being and feelings moment by moment.**

E. Our default setting is well-being

Remember that we are meant to feel good and we are designed to naturally flow in well-being. This is our default position as human beings. If you are unsure whether this is true, then take a look at young children. They still remember that they are here to feel good, have fun, and be enthusiastic about things they choose to like. They know how to feel good and, given a choice, will run around showing their joy and happiness easily. They can switch from crying to laughing in a moment without wanting to hold judgment.

All too often, we learn to bring in resistance to well-being and upload all sorts of reasons to feel bad, telling ourselves stories about what is going wrong and how bad things have become. Give yourself a day off from this approach and allow yourself to feel good no matter what.

Do it today. And then do it again tomorrow. And repeat this daily.

Notes:

....

....

....

GPS

F. Inner GPS

You have a magnificent internal GPS–a Genius Pointing System, if you will–which never fails. As part of building your intuition, which is here to guide us emotionally in life, you need to increase awareness of this internal navigation system.

When we are feeling good inside, it means that we're heading in the direction of our desires. When we are feeling bad or low and have bad feelings inside our stomachs, then this is our bodies signaling that we are out of alignment with our hearts' desires and preferred directions. It is a genius system and one that we could do with tuning into much more carefully. By learning how to listen to the signs we are giving ourselves from the inside out, we can steer toward better decisions and, therefore, better outcomes much more easily.

If you are feeling bad, then you are pushing against the flow, and you need to adjust to feel better. If you are feeling good, then this is a signal to your mind that you are in line to go where you want to be heading. So choose to engage in activities that generate the feeling of experiencing what you want to create.

These are important signals in manifesting, and we must learn to listen to the signals given to us by our bodies. Manifesting–the art of deliberate creating–is all about lining ourselves up to be in correspondence with our hearts' desires and tuning into alignment to resonate with our desired realities. Our bodies are built to show us when we're not in tune or not lined up to our chosen radio stations of life. Simply, it's all about whether we are feeling good or bad.

G. Intuition

When you have bad feelings, listen and pay attention to the messages that are being shown to you. Know that you are being shown through your intuitive senses (which never lie) that you are out of alignment.

With this vital information, you can take the necessary steps to change things and reposition your internal compass to a place which will take you where you want to be.

Listen to your intuition, which is played out in the form of gut feelings. Sometimes things just do not feel right; learn to trust your intuition. It is on your side and a supporter of your team, and it's giving you

Notes:
....
....
....

> **Make a choice now about the emotion you are going to choose today.**

very important information on your direction. It will assist you in figuring out how to move through to your next best choices.

H. Choose a new set point

We all tend to have a natural set point for our states of being. In other words, these are the default positions that we usually come from day to day, in terms of our feeling states. These default positions continue to be reinforced daily, as we find more things showing up in our lives to confirm that our own set points are corresponding precisely to who we are choosing to be (whether we are choosing to be someone who is happy, sad, rich, or poor).

We all know people who are generally upbeat most of the time, and we also know people who tend to choose to stick to the bleak and gloomy side of life. These are the people who always find something to complain or moan about. They will find a negative slant on anything, even on the good stuff. We have all come across people like this.

You can change your set point and choose a new default position at any time, and it is a wise move to do this. In manifesting terms, and in terms of

My best emotions:

deliberately creating a wonderful life, it is essential to have a high vibration as your daily set point. In other words, it is crucial to come from a place of well-being and happiness in order to manifest well-being and happiness in your life all of the time. Think on this. There are many strategies for shifting into a new emotion and you will find examples and instructions for this in Part C of this book. Go through these any time and begin the practice of creating a new emotional set point for your life.

Notes:

....
....
....

Set point ...

Finding your new emotional set point. Fill out the answers to these questions as honestly as you can ...

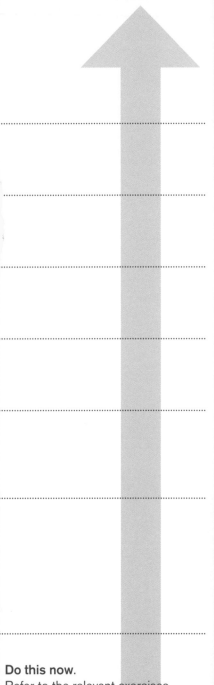

Do this now.
Refer to the relevant exercises
in Part C at this point if you
need help to achieve this shift.

Look again at the Emotions Chart and decide what your default position is right now.

Then, stop to ask two friends who know you well where they would place you on the scale. You may find the results surprising as we often fail to realize how negative or positive we appear to others.

Once you know this, you can begin moving up the scale to change your default position to a higher level, which will allow you to become a more deliberate creator of success, with a life to match.

You have to be feeling good to manifest positive things in your life. This is part of a universal law, the Law of Attraction.

Notes:
....
....
....
....
....
....
....
....
....
....
....
....
....
....

Finding your new emotional set point:

My default emotion up to now has been:

....

Friend 01's view of my default emotion up to now is:

....

I find this (e.g. wrong, surprising, interesting, spot on . . .):

....

Friend 02's view of my default emotion up to now is:

....

I find this (e.g. wrong, surprising, interesting, spot on . . .):

....

My new chosen default emotion is (e.g. happiness, forgiveness, feeling good, positive . . .):

....

To get to my target, I am working my way up the scale toward my new target emotional radio station starting with this emotion point (e.g. hopeful, optimistic, contented . . .):

....

Now, take your existing default emotion level and shift it to the new level that you have decided to work with on the chart.

Positive manifesting happens faster from higher states of emotion.

I. Emotions affect your reality

When you are in a low state of vibration, it can be difficult to do many things well or even to do anything well. You may feel heavier and have feelings of "being stuck."

When you're in a higher state of vibration and emotion on the scale chart, then you are able to communicate better, feel better, and do things better. It is likely that you will be feeling lighter and freer and it is at this level that ideas and creative thoughts flow freely and actions can appear effortless.

Use the negative signals as a way of identifying which areas of life you need to work on and adjust.

My happy places:

They are useful indicators in this respect. Then, move on quickly to find the better feelings.

It is so much easier to access creativity, inspiration, well-being, confidence, and insight when you feel good and you are running on a high-frequency wave band. All of these positive qualities resonate at the higher vibration, and it is easy to access this level when your emotions correspond to the high frequency.

Positive feelings allow us to access our own higher realms and resources, which are, in fact limitless.

Success requires good feelings.

As you can see, there is a compelling argument for aiming to maintain better states of being. It's the only route to being successful; you cannot have predominately negative feelings and find true success in life.

This book is aimed at getting you to journey to the good places inside yourself, easily and effortlessly. The next chapter gives you important information that will enable you to let well-being fly into your life fast and direct.

Notes:
....
....
....

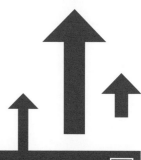

Chapter 4 checklist

Positive states of being are essential for happy creating ☐

Shift your current emotional state upward, step by step ☐

Avoid negativity and toxic conversations or any judgment of others ☐

Choose an environment that makes you feel good and strong ☐

You are the designer of your feelings, no one else ☐

We are meant to feel good ☐

Use your internal GPS for making decisions; it never lies ☐

Notice your default set point and shift up the scale to a better place ☐

Positive outcomes require positive feelings and states of being ☐

Emotion affects your reality and life experience 100% ☐

Notes:

....

....

....

Align

> ## To allow ourselves to let in beautiful lives full of our hearts' desires, we must vibrate effortlessly with joy, love, and wonder.

We are vibrational beings and we are designed to think, feel, and be. Our think/feel/be aspects dictate who we are and who we become, as well as what flows into our experience.

It is only by choosing feelings of joy that we create vibrant, successful, and happy lives. Want to know the good news? These are our default feelings as human beings. We just have to allow these default settings to reset.

A. Feeling good
As human beings, we are designed to feel good; we are meant to feel good. We are built and start out life configured as receptors of well-being. Often, we spend a good part of our early years reconfiguring our default positions and learning to load in fear, worry, and other negative aspects of being. Educational formats and parenting approaches often play a leading role in these moves toward the negative.

But how do we go about doing this? **The answer is in *alignment*.** We bring an alignment of energy vibration into our lives and we go about aligning with the versions of ourselves that we choose to be. What does this mean? Read on to find out.

B. "Many Worlds" model
In 1957, a physicist named Hugh Everett III created the "Many Worlds" model, following ideas coming out of the Copenhagen School of Physics. Widely accepted in the scientific

Notes:
....
....
....

Align

world, this model puts forward the idea that there is a multidimensional highway of infinite interconnected possibilities and realities.

The "Many Worlds" model proposes that this infinite number of realities already exists. The idea flows that we simply go about choosing a different reality from the many that are already on offer and that already exist simultaneously.

In the quantum field, the "Many Worlds" model reasons that there are many versions of us already in existence, as different versions of ourselves, but that we are only aware of there being one reality in our consciousness for the purposes of feeling present in our lives as they are.

Being aware of only one reality we are more able to focus on our experiences, learnings, and enjoyment of life.

For the purposes of our journey here, the "Many Worlds" model is a very useful tool for manifesting great things fast.

While honing our skills of deliberate creation, this model is useful for adopting the viewpoints that will help us manifest new outcomes and new versions of ourselves.

By using the "many versions" of reality model when applying the shifting and aligning techniques, we can more easily imagine shifting into new versions of reality. You get the idea of shifting into a new you more easily if you use a "Many Worlds" viewpoint.

So, consider reality creation in this way for now—you are not creating something from scratch that doesn't exist yet. Rather, you are moving and aligning into a new self that already exists and is available to you by simply choosing it. This makes the whole process seem so much easier and involves less work for us to do.

Compare it to going to a grocery store and seeing the range of different foods on the shelves and making a choice that is different from yesterday. Or slipping on a new pair of shoes that are better than the ones you have in your closet.

You are invited to use this model or framework as a way of thinking about the possibilities of reality creation. What is important is getting our minds to accept new ideas easily, and this "many worlds and many

Notes:

....

....

....

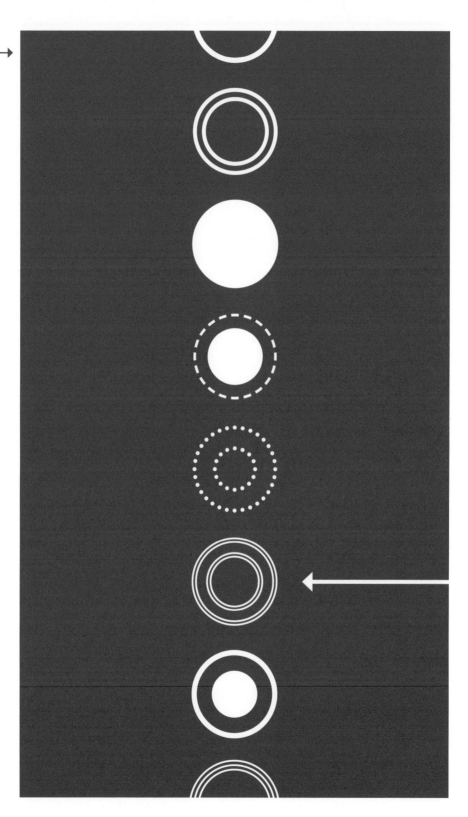

What we manifest and create in life emanates from our "being" choice and the version of us which we are choosing to be.

Step-by-step alignment with your chosen self

≡ Align

01. Choose a version of you that you want to be (healthy, wealthy, toned, happy, great job, family, whatever components you want to include for the you that you are choosing to be).

02. Go inside by closing your eyes and breathing to get relaxed. While in a relaxed state, instruct yourself to "align" with your chosen version. See or imagine or sense this new version within yourself and "step into it." Put this new "you" on, like a new suit, as the new version of who you are. Come from this place: breathe, feel, talk, walk, and make decisions from this new being space.

03. Get the feeling that you are in alignment with this new version of you. Come out, open your eyes, stay in alignment. This is the new version of you that you are being.

04. Go, have fun, and do what it is that you would be doing—only this time do it from the perspective of the new you.

Notes:

versions of being" model offers a great framework for this. **Let's go forward with this in mind.**

C. Align with a new version of you

Alignment is when you line up with who you are choosing to be in the present moment. You can choose to be any version of yourself you like and it could be the one who experiences the life you choose. Through your mind's alignment with your chosen self, your reality is created.

D. How do you align?

First, you mentally choose a version of yourself in full Technicolor detail, including any micro information you would like to add to this mix. Incorporating the fine details makes the exercise more effective.

Once you have chosen this, you step into this new version of "I" as if it

is who you really are, and then you come from this place in all aspects of your being. You breathe, act, think, feel, and be this version of yourself that you choose and then you discover that all experiences come to you to conspire to bring this version into play.

This may sound hard because of its simplicity but that's what it really is: simple and really easy. A child can do this and does so all the time while playing. So can we.

The idea is that, from this point of total alignment with your chosen version of you, you will come across the experiences that this version of self has already called into action. It is straightforward and it couldn't be easier to do. You do it often already, only this time you are going to do it consciously and with a focused intention of doing it.

Visualization: "Re-version"

Try this new set of "being-clothes" on now. Do you like the style and feel of this new you, now that you have tried it on? Examine it to see if it can be improved upon in any way. Any changes needed? If so, just make any adjustments to the version of you that you are aligning with, and align again.

Now, how is it? Do you like the new version of you? Does it feel good? The answer should be yes. Keep changing it until you get a resounding YES! Now you are looking good.

Audio 04: This audio is designed to show you how to align to a new version of you.

🎧 Audio

$$\text{Alignment} \ \times \ \frac{\text{your chosen version of you}}{\text{focus}} = \text{Allowing} \rightarrow \text{manifesting your dreams}$$

E. How do you know that you are aligned correctly?

Our emotions are the indicators of how aligned we are. If we are feeling good, then we are in alignment with who we are choosing to be. If we feel bad, then we know that we are not in alignment with our best, chosen version.

Use your emotions as a guidance tool that lets you know when you need to shift and make new, better choices and better alignments. The emotion system is engineered brilliantly to give you valuable and quality-controlled information fast. Bad feelings can be incredibly useful if we take notice and use them as helpful feedback in our lives, and make the changes necessary to move in a different direction toward happiness and joy.

Keep aiming for good feelings. This is the secret to success and positive, deliberate creation. Choose well. You get to decide your own emotions at all times. **So decide to feel good in this moment.**

Chapter 5 checklist	
"Be, feel, think" states dictate what shows up in our lives	☐
Joy is a key component of success	☐
We are well-being receptors and our default position is feeling good	☐
When deciding who you are, choose a great version	☐
Align with the chosen version of who you are being	☐
Be the success and joy you want in your life	☐
Emotions give us the truth about how strongly we are in alignment with our happiness and well-being	☐

Ask

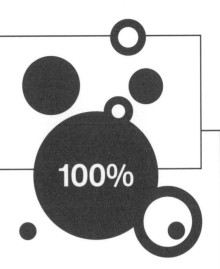

This idea has massive implications.

100%

If someone was to ask, *"What is the 'Holy Grail' in manifesting?"* I would reply along these lines: everything (and I do mean everything) that we ask for in our lives is responded to and answered by the universal energy with an affirmative. This includes what we call in with our words, thoughts, feelings, and mind chatter. All of these things go into the melting pot as instructions for what we are creating in our lives today.

The universal energy does not judge or filter these requests. There is no board of directors sitting in a meeting room at HQ, considering the requests and filtering out the ones that we don't really mean. *"Oh, he doesn't really want that; he has been on about having no money all his life. We don't believe that's what*

he wants really, so we will pull back on that request and not sanction it because we know it won't make him really happy."

No. This is not how it works.

> **You get precisely what you ask for.** You get it in full, with a receipt and guarantee, and this continues for the rest of your life. No judging, no discriminating. And you get it 100% of the time, without fail. It can feel like it takes a while, but it will always show up. **It is Law.**

A. Ask to receive

Now, if we accept that this is the case (and it is), would it mean that we would then decide to think, feel, or vibrate differently, say different things, or spend time with different

Notes:

....

....

....

Ask

Part A

> ## The majority of people do not believe that we can have anything we choose, yet we can.

people? Would it mean that we would choose to have only positively focused conversations? You bet.

Does it mean that we would stop moaning about what is wrong in our lives and start examining and focusing on what is right and what we are calling for in our lives?

Would we begin to tell the story of how we would like it to be rather than how it has been?

Would we choose to stop complaining and get on with it?

Would we turn off all the bad news coming at us?

Yes, yes, yes, yes, yes, and yes.

Does this resonate and make sense to you? It makes perfect sense in the realm of creating the life you want by manifesting good things and making life happy, fast.

If we followed the logic through, then we would stop trading gossip and bad news stories with one another and spend more time giving, pleasing, laughing, and dreaming up what we would like to bring in next. We would talk about things in

relation to how we want them to be. We would be keeping an eye out for things that correspond to our wishes and be more focused on taking the first step toward bringing our dreams into reality.

So, for example, if you would like a new car, then the manifesting route would be to have a look at some car dealers and car magazines, focus your attention on the vehicles going by, see what you like the look of and begin your plan to bring this to fruition. It would not be telling all of your friends how you desperately need to get some new wheels but haven't got a chance because you just do not have enough money.

Beat the drum on what you are choosing to bring about by having focus, positive attention, and taking small steps—leading to bigger steps—in the right direction.

In fact, everything we already have in our lives, we have chosen. This is true. What we think, feel, and believe is what we experience.

Our life is an elaborate display of our belief systems and our choices of focus; it is displayed for all to see. It really is that simple.

Notes:

....

....

....

If we took, say, Richard Branson as an example, we can declare with absolute certainty that he has positive belief systems around generating business and money. Many wealthy people have lost their money, only to regain huge sums again very quickly. The mind-set and belief systems about being wealthy are there for all to see. A common denominator in most rich people's thinking is that, if they were to lose all their wealth, they believe they would find a way to get it back quickly and become wealthy again. There are many examples that show this to be true. When the richest people in the world are asked what would happen if they lost it all, they believe they would get it back again and fast. They have the mind-set of *"I can make money easily."*

B. Leading a happy life

We lead happy lives by focusing only on the good stuff we want more of. What do we do about the bad stuff that comes in? Well, it gets dealt with quickly; don't engage in it or keep telling the story of it. Remove it from your life in the fastest way possible and move on.

This sounds very easy. It is and it isn't, all at the same time. It depends on your way of looking at it.

Life does throw out difficult and challenging stuff. Our job is to navigate through it and learn how to stay good inside, regardless of what is going on around us. We are presented with challenges to power us up and to learn important lessons.

Everything that happens we create through our mind work. Our greatest challenges become our greatest teachers in life.

If we have miserable adventures appearing in our lives, we need to take a look at our belief systems and mind program, as there will be specific beliefs running to make us believe we have to have these sort of things in our life, for one reason or another. We may have picked these beliefs up along the way from our parents or even our ancestors. It doesn't matter too much where they came from. The more useful question for us is: *"How do we change them?"*

C. It's all our own doing

Full responsibility for everything that we experience springs up from the idea that we *"ask"* and it is *"done."* When we ask for things in our lives, we must make sure that we ask in the positive and not give out a call for the negative: *"I never have*

Notes:

....

....

....

Ask

We did it, we created it all.

enough money; I need more." This statement resonates lack, need, and desperation. This sends out a vibration and a direct call for more "not having" what you want.

A better approach is to present ideas in terms of what you do want and ask for things positively and with gratitude: *"I am ready to receive more money and wealth into my life. Thank you."*

"I am now going to look at steps to make this work and look for everything in my life that supports me on this quest." This will line you up, give clarity to exactly what you are asking for in life, and stop the negative calling.

Talk to yourself, your mind chatter, your internal visualizing machine, your emotions, and your friends, in a positive manner. Speak only about the good stuff and not the bad. This is not telling lies. This is good reality creation and excellent management of your mind activity.

D. Taking full responsibility
Everything we have, we created with our minds. If you are experiencing negativity right now, know that mind power created it. No one else is to blame. So if you are someone who takes delight in bragging about how bad things are right now, stop it at once as this will create more of the same. Take responsibility for this fact.

Instead, talk about how the good things are getting better and how they already are better. Filtering your talk to start seeing things in this way will transport your life into much better harmony all around and will be your fast track to success and a happier life.

E. Manifesting
This know-how around mind power allows us to consciously use this powerful yet simple system for being able to call in precisely what we want in life. We can work with the magnetic nature of thought for our own life design and attract precisely what we choose. The more we come to understand that we are one—that we are part of the infinite nature of the universe and the universe is part of us—then the more we get to deeply understand how we shape our own realities and outcomes. More precisely, we come to learn that we hold all the power for shaping our lives through our thinking processes. As we learn this, we accept full responsibility and we get to see that we are in the driver's seat.

Notes:

....

....

....

Seven life rules...

The rules to live by.
Simply incorporating these concepts into our lives will expand our happiness, our abundance, our wealth, relationships, and all aspects of living in spectacular ways.

06. Our default position is
    well being, happiness,
    and joy.

    We are meant to be
    this and we are designed
    this way.

    Only if we pinch ourselves
    off from our emotions—
    which are here to guide us
    to happiness—do we
    experience life as difficult.

07. Everything is possible
    through focus, attention,
    and mind mastery.

These concepts help us understand
our best approaches to leading
a joyful and abundant life. It's a
reminder to remain happy at all
times, regardless of what goes on
around us. We can create anything
and we do so through our thoughts,
feelings, and emotions.

7

We can shape our lives like putty in the hands of a sculptor. What we think, feel, and believe will manifest. That's the why it is: pure and simple.

Our thoughts and emotions are powered through our consciousness and determine our reality. These ideas show us the importance of our thoughts and feelings in relation to our reality experience. They show us how we create the shapes of the lives we end up experiencing by our focus in each moment of now.

What we think, focus upon, and consume—the ideas we consider, the conversations we take part in, the music we listen to, and the art we look at—all add up to affect our conscious awareness, attention, and attraction points for manifesting our life stories.

Notes:

....
....
....
....
....
....
....
....

Seven life rules:

01. We create our experience through our mind activity: thoughts, feelings, emotions, and focus.

02. Every request is heard and acted upon by the universal machine.

03. We get precisely what we ask for, every time, in perfect time.

04. We are responsible for 100% of every outcome that shows up in life.

05. As we are choosing our thoughts, our emotions are guiding us as to whether this is taking us in a positive or a negative direction.

    If we head for better feelings in each moment, our lives will improve.

    It is a law of nature.

100%

Ask precisely and you will receive back–100% of the time ☐

Be careful what you ask for–things come to you exactly as you ask for them ☐

Drop focusing on bad news and trading negative gossip ☐

Our current experience shows our belief systems ☐

Focus on the good stuff and what you choose to bring forward into life ☐

Choose to feel good even when challenges arise ☐

Our lives are our own responsibilities in every way–no one else's ☐

Take steps toward what you would like to create ☐

We create life with every thought ☐

Emotions are our guidance system to tell us if we are on the right track ☐

Tell a better story–filter for the good stuff ☐

You can be, have, or do anything ☐

Notes:

....

....

Ask

Law

Everything and anything is possible.

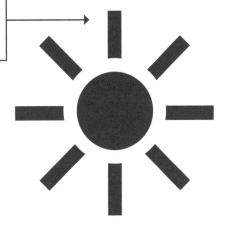

There are some irrefutable laws of the universe in operation which are relevant in any quest for happiness and success. These principles are set right into the heart of creating life the way you wish it to be. It is important to have an understanding of these laws in order to fully grasp how to manifest successfully in life.

The principles that you need to know to manifest positively are outlined here, in a way that allows you to gather insights into how the mind is set up to operate most powerfully. These universal laws provide an important context for success through conscious reality creation.

There are step-by-step directions in Part B on being the creating power-house for anything you choose.

A. The Law of Balance

Many people recognize what it's like to have mood swings and a range of feelings from being on top of the world to feeling in the depths of downheartedness or depression. People can experience many different levels of mood swings, and all of us have different emotions from time to time according to the rhythms and cycles of life.

Those who are mastering their emotions with deliberate conscious control bring into play the Law of Balance.

An important skill for a happy and abundant life is the art of staying balanced despite swings in feelings, and to know that these swings are just part of life. The secret here is to

Notes:
....
....
....

> **Our minds are infinite. Our powers are infinite. Our lives are infinite. Let's get excited.**

become an observer of the swings, rather than participating in the highs and lows of life, and positively reject the notion of changing your emotions from good to bad and back again. The best path is to keep feeling good, regardless of what goes on around you in life.

In other words: "Hold your emotions steady, whatever the weather."

This is a powerful tool, and those who master it are well on the way to becoming masters of deliberate creating.

The good news: we are all capable of this, regardless of what our beliefs are right now.

B. The Law of Potential

We are pure consciousness, all made of the same stuff, and when we realize that we have infinite potential, then we can line up easily with the power that creates everything. From here, everything is possible.

This powerful law reminds us that everything is possible for all of us, since we are creating everything through our consciousness and the nature of consciousness is infinite

potential. Our life, therefore, has infinite potential.

> The very nature of being a human being with an **infinite mind** allows us to access the power to create anything.

Get this. Breathe this idea in and feel the excitement of realizing this concept.

In order to get a sense of this law in action, all you have to do is take a walk outside in nature and open up your senses. Here we get the complete feeling of the abundance that is all around, simply by walking in nature. The expanse of the fields, flowers, air, sky, seeds, shoots, and the onward march of the seasons; all of these things are visual reminders that we live in a universe of infinite abundance. We are all made of the same stuff and we all have the same power and potential as the abundance seen in nature.

By meditating and going to the quiet space within and then feeling the expansion through our bodies, it is possible to notice and get the sense of our own connection to "all that is" and get a sense of the universe's infinite resources.

Notes:

....

....

....

Become an expert in both giving and receiving in balance.

It is pretty amazing being a human being anyway, and when you add in the idea that anything is possible, life starts to get really interesting.

It's all a miracle when you stop and think about it.

C. The Law of Giving

The universe works around the principle of giving and receiving in relation to the energy flow of life. The flow keeps flowing and as we give out, we receive. It is law.

Our world is dynamic and constantly changing. This is marked with the flow of life, by the seasons, night and day, life and death, and so on. The natural order of things involves both giving and receiving in life. This is one of the important keys to creating.

Just as blood and oxygen move around our bodies, our breath goes in and out and as day must follow night, so we must keep things moving in life. **We must flow in the balance of giving and receiving.** If we hang on to money and never let it go, then it will stagnate and clog up. Circulation is the key. In our relationships as well, we must give and take with balance in order to honor the flow and keep everything working for good.

It is true that the more you give, the more you will receive back. Anything we give out in life comes back multiplied, providing that it is given with a clear heart. It is all about the intention of giving and receiving that makes this law swing into positive operation.

The giving must be done purely, with a clear intention of truly giving, not in order to receive, but in order to spread the goodness and joy.

If it is money you are looking to attract into your life, then give some away. If it is joy you are after, give joy out to others randomly, including people you may not know. If you need love (and we all do, let's face it), then power out the love to others you come into contact with. If you need help, lend a hand and offer your help and services to someone who needs it.

This is a fast track trigger for the natural laws in creating more of the things you seek.

> **Give and receive** all good things every day for a healthy life and do so with good spirit and a **clear heart.**

Notes:
....
....
....

D. The Law of Karma

Every action generates a force of energy that returns to us in the same form, and often stronger. What we sow is what we reap. When we choose actions that bring happiness and success to others, then we receive the same back to our own lives in abundance.

Everything we do, good or bad, spins right back to us one way or another. The good deeds will come back to us multi-fold. So will the bad deeds. The same energy that we give out, comes right on back. Always, always, always.

Every choice we make in life has a consequence. The more we are able to become conscious of each choice we make, the more we are able to determine our own reality.

So, for example, if we want to experience a life of happiness and joy, we must sow the seeds of happiness and joy on our travels. Karma spins around the action of making conscious choices. Once we understand the concept of "we get back what we give out," then our conscious awareness becomes more directional and we learn to keep in the area of positive and good deeds only.

E. The Law of Paradox

There are many aspects of paradox running throughout the subject of reality and conscious creation. For example, there are differences between absolute truth and relative truths. Things appear real, while apparently also being an illusion.

Manifesting requires focus, and yet trying too hard to make things happen interrupts or can, in some cases, destroy the creating process. This is one of many paradoxical statements in manifesting and reality creation. This book will show you how to deal with this later.

For now, we will highlight the fact that, in our physical world of life experiences, there are many examples of paradoxes and we will refer to some of these along the way.

Knowing that paradoxes exist in many areas under the spotlight here, we can suspend our need to have fixed, firm, or absolute perspectives on some of life's big questions.

F. The Law of Ease

Nature works with ease and grace. The grass grows without any battles, the fruit ripens without a drama, everything works perfectly in nature

Notes:

....

....

....

—just as it should. In the same way, when we are lined up clearly for what we want, we create happiness and success with the effortless ease of nature's support.

> Allow yourself success **with ease**. Aim for this and all is well.

Miracles of nature occur without struggle. In nature we see that things flow, grow, and flower miraculously. When you watch how nature unfolds itself and proceeds through its natural course season by season, it is easy to see this law in operation.

When you come from a place of love, everything feels easy and effortless. When you have mastered a skill, you come at it free flowing and without resistance. When you do this with life in general, you gain mastery of the laws of the universe and of your own deliberate creation.

The Law of Ease teaches us:

01. Acceptance:
Learn to accept things are as they are, without judgment.

02. Responsibility:
Take responsibility for things that show up in life, as you have created your experiences according to your beliefs, thoughts, and emotions. Everything that shows up is here to show us important keys to life and to teach you important lessons.

03. Release blame:
Give up the need to blame others or to defend yourself; it's a waste of energy which is better used for positive creation. From a place of blame or being defensive, you are setting up a roadblock of resistance to desires and goodness coming into your life.

Relax into your position and know that you are OK being where you are. When you stop defending your position, there is no platform for arguments and disputes with others.

G. The Law of Intention
In every intention is the power for its fulfillment. If we can think it, it is possible. Intention in the field of infinite potential has infinite organizing power. When we introduce an intention in the ground of pure potential, we put this infinite organizing power to work fast.

Whatever we can imagine, we can create. Setting up intentions is the first phase to trigger manifesting.

Notes:

....

....

....

> # In order to acquire anything in the physical universe, we have to give up attachment to it.

If we add in desire, then suddenly the full potentiality of the universal delivery service is set in motion.

Put simply: first intend, then desire and know it's all possible—then watch the fireworks of success explode.

H. The Law of Detachment
In detachment we can become free from fear. In the place of uncertainty lies freedom from our pasts and from our beliefs. In our willingness to step into the unknown, the field of all possibility, we pass the control over to the infinitely creative part of our minds.

When working with this principle, the idea is that we keep our intentions or desires and then we simply *release any attachment to the result.* **This is as powerful as it gets.**

Attachment comes out of fear and insecurity and from a "lack" consciousness. Attachment is usually toward material symbols and carries with it feelings of being helpless, out of control, desperate, and fearful.

Detachment, on the other hand, is the basis of wealth consciousness and has built-in freedom in its own expression. It is associated with happiness, laughter, and ease. To truly go about experiencing wealth consciousness, we have to be grounded in the idea of the uncertainty and detachment to the outcome, and it's here where we will find the freedom to create anything we want.

By stepping into the unknown and letting go of any attachment to the desired outcome, we naturally step straight into the heart of pure potentiality and infinite possibilities. **This is the place from which things spring forth rapidly and easily.**

Those who are looking for security from money *itself* will never find what they're looking for. The wealthiest people are often the most insecure. This is because they hold fear around money and believe they need it to feel safe.

Embrace uncertainty and embrace the idea that it's OK for anything to happen.

Being in need with manifesting is the fastest way to freeze the free flow and stop things coming to you. We do not have to come up with the answers of how to get from A to B;

Notes:
....
....
....

this is the job of the universe. We simply have to define where we want to go and then give up the struggle and allow it to happen naturally. It is often delivered in ways that we could never imagine or dream up. Release feelings of need and trying to control outcomes.

Allow things to play out the best way, knowing that they will. When you are operating from detachment and uncertainty, solutions pop out easily and smoothly, allowing you to continue along your way happily. **This is the route for a fabulous life and ease of living.**

I. The Law of Purpose
We all have a purpose in this life—hidden or otherwise. We all have special gifts and talents to offer the world. When we find out what these are and work with them, offering ourselves in service to others and our communities, we radiate happiness, success, and well-being.

This law acknowledges that we all have unique gifts. It teaches us that we all have our own purpose. When we know what our talents are and we match them with our creative expression then our lives are activated into joy.

Expressing ourselves allows the creation of unlimited wealth and abundance. Doing what we enjoy and being the people we are born to be are the triggers for a meaningful life.

Make a list of your talents—no matter if these are small or large:

_____

_____

_____

_____

_____

_____

_____

_____

_____

_____

Make a list of the things you love to do:

_____

_____

_____

_____

_____

_____

_____

_____

_____

_____

_____

_____

Make a list of the things you would be doing if time and money were not important:

_____

_____

_____

_____

_____

_____

_____

_____

_____

_____

_____

_____

_____

Make a list of your purpose in life as you see it today:

If there were no limits, what would your purpose be?
Is it any different? Why?

How can I help others?

_____

_____

_____

_____

_____

How can I be in service to others?

_____

_____

_____

_____

_____

How can I help mankind with my gifts?

_____

_____

_____

_____

_____

_____

J. No "push" or force

In mindful creating, pushing too hard will interfere with the flow and create a block in the flow of the process.

By giving ideas or intentions a "push" with your mind, or using too much force, a resistance is set up. This blocking force, which is really backed by a fear of failing, can cause the complete blocking of a manifestation process.

How do we combat this? We use a light touch, gentle as a feather, and remove the need to "push" the thing into existence with our will.

Lightly, softly, and gently is the only way to go here. It won't work by using forceful thinking or a push mentality. Remember, the rule of thumb is that if you are pushing for it to happen, you are pushing it away.

K. Let go of willfulness

One of the most powerful things you can do to create anything, is to let go of the need to have that thing in your life. Drop the word "need" from your vocabulary. You can say instead that you "invite things in" or that you are "choosing" something specific. This is much better language for positive creating.

Notes:

....

....

....

Making it OK to fail in your quest for creating

Release all need. If you "need" something to happen, and believe that this something must happen for you to be OK, then fear is in operation and this fear will be the very thing that pushes it away. So, by heavy "needing," you end up with the opposite of what you have been aiming for.

Too much need and willfulness being present is one of the reasons why much Law of Attraction work—simply presented—does not work for some people. It's one of the elements explaining why people can so easily fail on their conscious creation path.

This won't happen to you as you are learning all of the additions to the Law of Attraction process and being given the information you need to manifest successfully. In addition, you are being inoculated against blocking the laws as we go through this work.

> Come at your manifesting choices with a **relaxed disposition** and without need, fear, or attachment to the outcome and success is yours.

L. Make it OK to fail

For successful manifesting of any kind, we need to make it OK in our heart for us not to receive what we are asking for. This is a paradox, of course, as is the case with many aspects of manifesting.

By making it OK to fail in your quest for something in particular, you are allowing any fear to dissolve away and, in so doing, removing negative blockages to the attraction process.

Our lives are perfect as they are. We don't actually need anything else; we already have the right blend of life for where we have chosen to be right now. Use this as a template when applying the "making it OK to fail" frame of mind to whatever it is that you are manifesting.

This may sound confusing, and it may feel strange at first. Many times I have asked my clients to make it OK to fail in the thing that they want to manifest. This is usually a very difficult thing for people to do; many struggle with this. Yet once they are able to accept this inside and make it truly OK in their hearts for them not to pull off the manifestation, then somehow something shifts inside. The fear goes away. The push energy retreats. The softness comes in and leaves a pure intention there. Ironically, it is often at this point the manifestation shows up—right on time.

Notes:

....

....

....

01. Choose your theme

Choose something that is not yet in your life that you would deeply and strongly like to have. Choose something that has a strong emotional charge to it.

02. Relax, release, and breathe

Close your eyes and relax. Think of the thing that you choose to manifest. Now consider not getting it at all for a moment.

Notice where the energy disturbance travels through you and view it as an observer. Release this energy disturbance by saying to yourself, *"I am choosing to release and let go of this need now"* and breathe deeply, allowing the release inside. The deep breathing will automatically allow you to release, let go and relax, as long as you allow it to do so. Feel the energy move through your body and simply allow the feeling to move on through.

Let the energy move up and out of your body and, as it moves, notice the shifting of energy that takes place inside your body. This may be a fizz, a tingle, or a very gentle sensation, but you will notice it when it moves.

Now consider again making it OK to fail with your chosen intention. If you still have resistance or any sort of anxiety, come up again, notice it move through you, and feel it gently release out further each time. Keep on doing this releasing step until there is no more resistance. You may do this a few times or many times to get it all released.

Repeat this over and over until you are able to make it feel OK for the thing not to happen after all. Just make it OK. Get yourself to feel that your life is going well anyway, whether or not you get this thing you would like in your life.

03. Feeling free and comfortable no matter what

You will reach a point after fully releasing this energy inside where you can relax and be free and comfortable in yourself whether or not your intention comes into being. The ultimate feeling of inner freedom is to know that you are really safe and secure, no matter what transpires in life.

You have now cleared a blockage to manifesting in this area of your life. Magical things will start to appear once you have released on any powerful blocker like this. Congratulations! By doing this process in full, you have unblocked your fears.

Now, full steam ahead with successful creating.

Often we get delivered far more than we dared to ask for.

Chapter 7 checklist ☑

Laws of paradox, balance, potential, giving, karma, ease, intention, detachment, and purpose ☐

Know your purpose ☐

Let go of willfulness ☐

Our current experience shows our belief systems ☐

Do not be attached to outcome ☐

Make it OK to fail ☐

Notes:

....

....

....

The instructions

Here are clear no-nonsense instructions on the manifesting process. Follow the instructions carefully and with precision. All of the information you will need to understand about how to create any life experience is here. It is necessary to understand all of the information from Part A in order to complete Part B successfully. Realize now that whatever you choose to think and feel determines precisely what shows up in your life. Everything you experience has already been summoned through your unconscious to become present in your conscious experience. Realize now that everything is here to show you how to create the life of your dreams, easily, effortlessly, and with absolute certainty. The instructions work in practice, if you follow the given rules, 100% of the time.

Create

CREATE

Calm

Relax

Experience

Ask and Allow

Thanks

Effortless Expectation

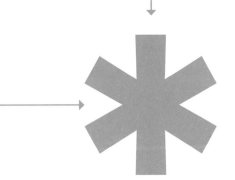

A. CREATE instructions

Here are the instructions for abundant manifesting and purposeful creation. Follow these steps carefully. Each step is essential. None of the steps may be left out. Master the details by reading them several times over and getting them clear in your mind.

Set it–forget it–flow from it–be it   Create

Summary
Choose the theme of what you would like to manifest into your life. Make it clear and simple. Then do the following:

C: Calm
Establish a profound state of calm and centeredness inside yourself. Begin by closing your eyes and thinking about everything that you are grateful for already and all of the wonder that you have in abundance in your life now. Feel yourself centered and present inside your body. Feel "you" inside yourself and notice the feeling.

R: Relax
Continue from this feeling into a relaxed, peaceful, quiet, meditative state. Breathe deeply.

E: Experience
Allow yourself to experience and accept the new "being" state of having this manifestation already in your life. Do this by imagining and feeling it already happening.

A: Ask and Allow
Now ask precisely and clearly for the thing that you are calling for and imagine allowing this into your life. Get the feeling of

accepting it as it flows into your experience easily.

Ask: *"I ask, allow and accept that I already have .... in my life and I have the feelings and experience of already having this."*

Ask to receive. Align with the version of you that knows and has the experience of already having this. Accept this version of you and be it now.

Sit comfortably in this new place. Come from the place of already "being" this person and feel that you already have the manifestation present in your life.

T: Thanks
Immerse yourself in thanks. Offer huge amounts of gratitude and appreciation to trigger the positive powers of the Law of Attraction.

Say this: *"I give thanks for this, or something better, already being present in my life, in the best way. I have faith in this."*

Add: *"Thank you. It's done. Show me."*

Observe what you see in your mind's eye.

A sense of a "message sent receipt" can come into awareness at this point. Watch out for this as a sensation around your mind's eye marked by a flash, a feeling, or a sensation indicator of some kind.

E: Effortless expectation
Release any sense of "pushing," willfulness or attachment to the outcome.

Know with absolute certainty that it is already done and float into the "being" sense of having it in your life already. Be the person who already has this—act like it, breathe like it, feel it, and be it.

Once you have followed these steps, simply move onward with your day. Proceed with a new version of you and with a clear release of any feelings of attachment to the outcome. Let it all go. Forget about it, and let it be free to move.

Set it—forget it—flow from it—be it

Notes:

....

....

....

B. Details

Now to get you tuned in fully with these principles, we will go through the process point by point and fill in the details.

01. Calm

First of all, it is important to establish a positive state of calm, centeredness, and abundance inside. Seeing life through a frame of calm, centered abundance will set up the right environment for quality manifesting. This is done by going inside and noticing and acknowledging what you already have in your life and giving thanks for all of it. This is the trigger to becoming truly, profoundly abundant.

It is much easier and faster to energize and to attract more abundance to you from a position of already *feeling* and *being* abundant. More of any "state-of-being" creates and attracts more of the same vibration, so begin by setting your vibration to a high abundance state from the start.

How do we do this? Begin by noticing how grateful you are for all the good things in your life. Each person will have different things on their list; it may be

gratitude for your health, children, your partner, the joy from a hobby, your job, your family, living in clean air, a safe home, good friends, a sense of humor, someone doing you a kind service unexpectedly, being able to help someone with practical service or advice, your pet, a smile you received, thanks given to you in kind . . . you get the picture. When you start doing this, you realize there is so much to be grateful for, and usually in the most simple areas of life.

If you first think you haven't got anything in your life to be grateful for, look again or even make it up for now. Begin somewhere and get rolling with it. This will help you see through abundant eyes and give you the clarity of appreciation, which will help you generate more abundance.

> **Daydream to get a clear picture of the things that you choose to bring into your life.** Imagine seeing your dreams come true with insight and clarity.

02. Relax

Get into a peaceful, quiet, relaxed, meditative state. Being in the right state will allow you to process the instructions faster and more

Notes:
....
....
....

profoundly. It will also allow you to easily connect with the manifesting space within.

There are a number of different ways to get into this "peak" state where manifesting will be a breeze. Here are a few guidelines for helping to get yourself into the best state for manifesting:

i. Follow the **audio visualizations** that accompany this book. They will take you easily into a calm state of abundance.

ii. Learn to meditate and achieve inner calm by going into a deep relaxed state easily with daily practice. Get instruction on how to meditate correctly. This is one of the most useful tools for successful manifesting. I have used Transcendental Meditation for years and it is one of the greatest tools in having a successful life. It helps you connect easily and regularly to the inner bridge that leads you into manifesting your dreams fast.

iii. Close your eyes and go inside. Breathe and relax to access a meditation-like state of being. Keep breathing and going deeper

down inside, relaxing more as you do so. Begin to access the floating feeling of relaxation and go deeper in with each breath. Do this for five to ten minutes before continuing with the manifesting method. Not only is this a lovely thing to do, it will also put your mind into a peak state to receive your manifesting instructions.

Train your brain to go into a deep relaxed state using one of the relaxing methods above. Going into these deeper states allows increased connection to the manifesting triggers. You may consider following a course which teaches how to access these brain wave states at higher levels, although you can manifest perfectly well by simply using the frame of reference that you are already abundant, and then going into a deep state of relaxation. Listening to a soundtrack of relaxing music or meditative sounds in the background will also help get you into a good relaxed state.

03. Experience
From a calm relaxed state and a feeling of abundance, allow yourself to come from a place of already experiencing what it would be like to have the thing you are choosing.

Notes:
....
....
....

Act as if you have it, think and feel as if it is already there, and create your feelings from the position of a person who already has this showing up in their life.

It is all about imagining that you are that person already—acting as, being as, walking as, feeling as, and thinking as them. Allow yourself to experience life from now on as though this manifest request is already in your reality right now.

You may say, "But isn't this living a lie? Isn't this being untruthful?"

No, this is about creating your reality by going there first in your *being state* and *feeling state* and *thinking state*. This is about consciously and deliberately creating your life experience in a harmonious way. We are meant to be in harmony, to have whatever we choose, and to be happy. This is the methodology. So do this, literally, to get the life you choose.

If you go to this place first in these states, then the reality will show up in your life. It is a law of the universe that if you hold the alignment and the being state of someone who has these things already, then you

will manifest them into your life. The attraction factor kicks in from the vibrational sense that you create in this moment.

This is so because of laws of the universe: **it works whether you believe it or not.**

Remember we are vibrational transmitters of frequency and we are constantly transmitting through how we are choosing to feel and what we imagine. This is received and acted upon by the magnetic nature of the universe.

So go ahead. Just begin by accepting and allowing and being the version of you that already has this experience showing up in your life.

04. Ask and Allow

Now ask for precisely what you wish to experience in your life. It is important to word your intention clearly and positively and to ask for precisely what you are choosing to bring in. State this in the positive position, make it unambiguous, and add detail, as the universe is not about interpreting or filling in the gaps— it provides precisely what you're asking for.

Notes:

....

....

....

So for example, to say *"I ask, allow, and accept that I already have lots of money"* is pretty much an impossible concept to satisfy without specification or speculation. What is *"a lot"*? (Are we talking 10¢, $10, or $10 million?) Without a specifier, this is too vague a concept for what we want to achieve here. It is necessary to state things in a way that is as *precise* and as *specific* as possible.

Make your instruction in the present tense, include your name to anchor it to you, and position the it as a direct request, stated in the positive and in the now.

Next, *align* with the version of you that already has this experience present in your life.

> Take on alignment of **being this person who already has it** and *BE the version of you who already has it* now.

05. Thanks
Next, give thanks and gratitude for having this outcome already in your life. Giving thanks and feeling appreciation is the fastest way for your mind to resonate and vibrate as abundant, thereby attracting and creating more of this in your life. Feel grateful for all things and give thanks for the manifesting outcome having already happened. It is impossible to have a negative attraction factor running while you are expressing and feeling gratitude and appreciation for things in your life.

> **The words to say are:**
> *"I give thanks for this, or something better, already being present in my life, in the best way. Thank you. It's already done. Show me."*

The observer
"Show me" in the above statement allows the observing aspect of the command to be included. This is necessary to activate the manifesting instruction to take form in reality.

From quantum theory, we know that an observer is required to make any event in space come into the form of reality.

The observer aspect of the process in the "show me" command provides the instruction to your inner being to be the observer of the shift and to witness acceptance of the command on the universal platform. This brings the shift into your perceived reality.

Notes:

....

U Attract ....

....

It's physics. Trust me: we have it on good authority from leading scientists of our time that this is true.

When the instruction is accepted, you may notice some white flashes or shots of little lights in the "third eye" area of your mind (the space located between your eyebrows just behind your forehead). This is you observing the changes being made at a quantum and physical level. It is a witnessing of the movement of light from cells. Similar to small-scale fireworks, the appearance is like the stars you can see on a clear night, only this time the stars and bright lights appear to fire off around your mind's eye area.

Message Sent receipt: "the clunk"

> To witness these firing stars or lights inside your mind after you issue your instructions is like an *e-mail sent* receipt to show that the instruction has been sent and activated.

Once you have observed the instruction being fired off, you can feel a "clunk" when it falls into place, like a "message sent" receipt—a feeling that tells you the instruction has been sent successfully.

This feeling can be like a click or a gentle shifting, or a gentle clunk—and can be accompanied by a feeling of absolute certainty that it is done. This aspect sometimes only happens to more advanced students of manifesting.

Aim for this feeling of the message sent receipt, the feeling of the click or the clunk, a signal to you that it is done and complete.

Once you get this, it is reassuring and a great feeling. I will never forget the first time I noticed this; it was a "wow" moment in my life the first time I felt the "clunk" kick in. I didn't know what it was at the time; I just knew it was a signal that the manifest was a done deal and I had a feeling of certainty that this is what it was telling me.

Simply notice it when it comes. Do not try or be willful to get it; this will push it further away. It will come at the perfect time for you. It is subtle, but nevertheless, it signals one of the most powerful mechanisms in the universe: the successful creating power of your mind.

With this full knowledge, you can create anything in your life.

Notes:

....

....

....

Rules for wording instructions

Remember that each person gets to decide their own thoughts and feelings at all times. We have the potential only to affect our own lives through deliberate creation. We do not have the right to control others or to affect the free will of other people.

01. It must be a clearly worded instruction

02. Use the name you are commonly known by in the statement

03. It must be worded as if it is happening in the present

04. The instruction should be presented as already being in your life

05. Include thanks for already having it

06. Be clear, unambiguous, and specific; you get precisely what you ask for so be careful about how you phrase it

07. Include the "show me"/observer aspect to fire up the form into reality

Notes:

....

....

....

"......................................
....
....
....
....
....
......................................"

OK

06. Effortless expectation

Be comfortable and relaxed, and release any "push" or controlling mentality in this process. Any push or willful exertion or attachment to the outcome will make the procedure invalid and useless.

This may sound contradictory or too difficult, but you must get this idea. You do not need to push to make anything happen. Instead, it is a gentle intention setting, a lightness of touch in all of the processes.

> Make it OK for the manifesting outcome **not** to happen.

This is an odd request, yet it is a very important piece of the puzzle. Here's why:

What does this "make it OK for it not to happen" mean? It means that you need to give up any insistence or desperation around the fact that this outcome must happen for your life to be OK.

With this sort of idea running through your mind there will also be fear, anxiety, and a strong negative current present too, which will potentially switch off the positive attraction and turn on the negative.

All fear, anxiety, or push must, therefore, be let go. Allow it to be OK for this command not to be brought to fruition; then, the fear or the control aspect will dissolve, leaving you free to easily manifest the positive.

The thing to do is not to mind either way. Let go of any fear. Let go of any controlling urge. Just let go and be free with whatever outcome arrives, knowing that this is perfect for you at this time in your life.

You will then be operating from a place of neutral harmony, which is the best ground for manifesting your choices and desires.

This whole section may sound contradictory—it is not. It is a key component of the knowledge of how to manifest successfully. Go with it.

Practice letting go of any attachment to the outcome so that you really do not care one way or the other. Feel this in your emotional center and know this in your thought center.

Once you have let go of attachment to outcome, relax and enjoy yourself in the certain knowledge that everything comes in effortlessly and perfectly. . . and it does so every time.

Notes:

....

....

....

Just move forward now, after completing these steps. Continue with your day and whatever everyday tasks there are for you to do. It may be the simple things like going to get groceries, doing a work project, or watching a video. Whatever it is, just go onward and proceed from this new version of you, the "being state" of you, who already has the manifest thing present in your life.

Float off forward, get into your day, forget about the manifesting process, and move on happily, knowing all is perfect.

C. Summary

Calm:
Create a feeling of calm and an inner state of abundance by noticing what you have already.

Relax:
Get into a relaxed, quiet state by going inside and breathing deeply into quietness.

Experience:
Allow yourself to experience having the thing already and your new "being" state.

Ask and allow:
Ask and allow in order to receive. Allow it in and accept it. Align with the new version of you, who already has it. Be it and come from the space of having it already.

"I, (add your name), ask, allow, and accept that I already have .... in my life and I have the feelings, wisdom, and experience of already having this."

Thanks:
"I give thanks for this, or something better, already being present in my life for the best."

"Thank you. It's done. Show me."

Observe what you see. Notice the firing and sprinkling of star like lights in your third eye area if you can. Get the "clunk" sensation of sent/received mental mail.

Effortless Expectation:
Release any push, willfulness, or attachment to the outcome in your approach. Relax in effortless certainty. It is a universal law that "as you ask, it is given."

Now simply get on with things in your day. Let go of all willful intentions and push; release and allow it all to free-flow into form.

Set it—forget it—flow from it—be it

 Create

"Coincidence" is manifesting in action.

D. Notes

01. Be clear about your true desire

It is rarely "the money" (for example) we actually want in our lives; rather, it is the feeling of freedom we get from being in a place of financial independence. It may, therefore, be more appropriate to ask to create the condition of feeling free and independent to follow your own course in life and make new choices as you wish—rather than asking for money, for example. Money can come and go, while if you go for the condition and the feeling state as your request, it is likely that you will benefit from a life well lived through choice, freedom, and a continuous flow of all the good stuff.

02. Maintain privacy around your desires

Do not discuss your choices and desires with others; instead, keep them private. If you open up debate and invite other points of view, things get distorted and negative comments can come in which easily disrupt your flow. It's better to keep these things private or between you and your personal mentor, if you have one.

03. Notice synchronicities

Manifesting creates amazing synchronicities, which sometimes are so far-fetched that they can seem laughable and almost unbelievable. You will start to notice more of these things appearing in your life—chance meetings, the right person showing up with a solution, opportunities pouring in unexpectedly, and serendipity coming at you from surprising directions. Take note—make a record of these as this is manifesting at work in its highest form.

I love seeing the synchronicities appear after posting some manifesting creation requests.

> At the perfect time to bring your creations to life, the universe will conspire to bring you exactly what you need. Often you will see these in the form of the most amazing "coincidences." See them and smile.

04. Challenges come up along the way

Expect challenges and deal with them positively and swiftly. Keep in alignment with having the thing you are after already in your life, yet be aware that obstacles may come up as a test platform to stretch you and teach you more deeply important lessons.

Notes:

....

....

....

> **Everything that shows up is perfect, including the apparent hiccups and challenges.**

These challenges can come up simply to test your position—for example, to establish that you really do want what you have asked for—to test your alignment abilities, and also to provide lessons that you may need to absorb prior to receiving your request into your life.

Obstacles or challenges appearing along the path are not indications of failure. Simply notice them for what they are as opportunities to grow and learn more. In each challenge is a seed of opportunity for the growth and development of your understanding.

Investigate what you need to do in order to successfully step over them and learn what they are offering you, and **move on knowing that the challenge has presented itself for a good and positive reason.**

05. Expect the unexpected
Manifestations, more often than not, come from the most unexpected places and in more magnificent ways than we expect.

I am sure that you will have personal examples of this happening in your life already if you stop to consider this. Notice things working the way

you want them to and suspend the need to dictate the way in which the manifesting is served up to you; it probably will not be in the way that you would expect.

06. Ego tells you all the things about why change can't happen to you
If ego begins chattering about why this cannot happen because you are (take your pick)—

too old
too broke
too unlucky
too fat
too thin
too unlovable
too unworthy
too uneducated

—to have this, laugh at it. Ignore it and move onward, knowing that you are perfect and your manifestation will work.

07. You get to choose what you ask for—and the universe gets to choose how it gets served up.
Remember, it is not your job to work out how it happens. This is up to the universe to sort out. Your job is simply to state your desires and intentions clearly, profoundly, and positively, and align with this. The universe gets

Notes:
....
....
....

> **Have faith that it will work and do not get swayed in your faith and focus.**

to design the way that these are delivered to you.

08. Keep on with affirmations and visualizations to hold the right vibration

Use affirmations and visualizations to continue the vibration and the harmony of your chosen outcome within yourself. Use these techniques regularly and consistently to maintain the positive vibration of already having the things you choose in your life. This keeps the energy flowing and the attraction process continual; it also keeps the vibration constantly in alignment with the Law of Attraction, which means you are successfully moving in the desired direction.

09. Timing

Manifesting can happen instantaneously and does so in the quantum field. The energy of thoughts and emotions play out in the quantum field instantaneously, with immediate effects.

> Why then do our manifestations often take time to show up in our perceived reality?

There are a few reasons why this is so. One is that if everything that we wished for showed up immediately in our life, we would experience a great deal of chaos and confusion. In addition, we may need to do some work, have some experiences, or release some limiting beliefs before something can show up in our reality field easily, effortlessly, and perfectly.

There is a time lag sometimes between asking and receiving. On reflection, this is a great design.

We have to accept this and be patient, knowing that what we have asked for will indeed show up in our lives if we have followed the instructions carefully and provided that we are not sending out conflicting vibrational energy.

Be patient and allow the showing up of what you have called into your life at the right time and in the perfect way. Have faith in this. It will always show up providing that there are no conflicting beliefs or inner vibrations being sent out to prevent it.

E. Swerve the blockers

01. Complaining

Complaining is a fast shortcut for cutting off the routes to successful manifesting. This state contributes

Notes:

....

....

....

fast, negative attraction. It will keep you focusing on lack and the negative position, which will attract more lack into your life. This sets completely the wrong vibration and will ensure that the things you want do not arrive in your experience and that you continue experiencing the lack of them rather than the manifestation of them.

Drop the whining. **Bring up the gratitude and appreciation for all that is going right.** Find something that feels great, focus on that, and be thankful for it.

02. Judging or criticizing others

The acts of judging or criticizing others come from a position of fear and lack. These are the fastest ways to block goodness and prosperity from coming to you.

These activities are attractors for misery, emptiness, and fear, because these are the corresponding vibrations and emotions to judgment and criticism.

Rather, replace these unattractive and damaging traits with unconditional love, enthusiasm, and wholesale gratitude.

03. Making it OK to fail

It is important to make it OK to fail. Make it OK that a manifestation does not show up in your life, and know that you are still OK. This will take the sting and the potency out of the tail of fear, which is the number one blocker of manifesting positively.

Make it OK to fail and then move on with a positive frame, knowing all is well. This will help release fear from the process, leaving you to proceed on a clear path to success.

And so it is. Here you have learned the precise technique for visualizing and calling in anything you choose into your life, knowing for sure that you will have it show up.

This is powerful stuff. Use it wisely and use it for good. It can only be used in your own life and cannot be used for other people. Everyone has free will to do what he or she chooses in their own life.

The technique described in this section works 100% of the time if it is followed precisely.

It works. It works. It works.

Notes:

....

....

....

> Everything becomes
> possible from here.

You have full control of your mind and emotions. Your mind controls what shows up in your reality. The more you get into the zone of operating with these instructions, the more you will be living in joy, abundance, health, and vitality.

Audio 06:

Listen to this audio and be guided through this process.

The instructions are given here to take you directly into the space of manifesting and lead you step by step through the process.

I will be with you the whole way.

This audio will show you exactly what to do to create your own *Instructions for Happiness and Success.*

Let's go.

 Audio

Notes:

....

....

....

Chapter 8 checklist ☑

Follow each step carefully ☐

The techniques work 100% when followed precisely ☐

Practice the method regularly ☐

Release the need for any "push" or "pull" ☐

Observe what happens in your mind's eye ☐

Watch for the message-sent receipt ☐

Add faith, trust, and certainty to the process ☐

Make it OK for things not to happen ☐

Keep your manifesting details private ☐

Keep an eye out for the synchronicities ☐

If challenges pop up, step over them and move on fast ☐

Expect the unexpected ☐

Cut out complaining ☐

You get to choose what you want, not how it's delivered ☐

Once you're done, move on and flow with the day ☐

Expand

What's the good news? Negative programs are easy and fast to blast.

We have covered precisely how to go about creating whatever you want in your life through deliberate manifesting. Brilliant. Now what could possibly go wrong?

Well, there are a few things that can come up that will throw a monkey wrench into the works. By covering these now, we will avoid such roadblocks once and for all and ensure there is a clear path ahead to making great changes in your life.

Part of the road map for successful manifesting is upgrading your internal software. Here we are going to look at reorganizing limiting belief systems, develop an understanding about the power of the ego, and get ready to install some new frameworks that will support you at the highest level in achieving a successful life. These new frameworks will enable new changes to come into your life more easily.

This chapter is important to digest and work through carefully. It is necessary for us to lose limiting beliefs, blocks, and sabotage programs in order to manifest successfully. If we have negative programs running on top of our work then all of the good work running below will be worthless.

A. Free your mind
Many of us have had negative programs running for years. Sometimes these will have existed for longer than our own lifetimes, having been passed down from parent to child through the generations.

Notes:
....
....
....

Free your mind

Here are a few examples of other unhelpful programs we could be running:

For example, if you were brought up to believe "life is tough no matter how hard you try" then it will be. This belief may have been installed at an early age and could have been with you all your life.

- Life is tough / Life is difficult
- The bad guy always wins / The good guy never wins
- Money is always tight / I never have enough / I am always poor
- You can't trust anyone / People are out to do you wrong / Expect the worst / Things always go badly for me
- I can't keep a job / No one will hire me
- I have large bones, that's why I can't lose weight / I have fat genes so I can't lose weight / People hate me because I'm fat / I don't overeat, I'm naturally fat / Eating makes me happy / I can eat what I like: I don't care / I have always been fat
- I don't care what anyone thinks about me / Other people don't care / You don't care / Why should I care? / People hate me / No one likes me / No one listens to me / No one will help me
- I am not safe / Bad things always happen to me / I fear death / I fear success / I fear failure
- I fear a broken relationship / I fear my partner being unfaithful / Men are not to be trusted / Women are not to be trusted / Men are cheaters / Women are cheaters

These are just a few examples of the ideas that people may hold deeply in their internal belief make-up. Holding such beliefs will make it difficult or even impossible to create positive change in your life.

There are many methods to easily get rid of unhelpful beliefs, but the first step is to identify them.

Do this by focusing on the area of your life that you are looking to improve. In your chosen area of focus, **write down the things that hold you back.** Then, seriously review whether these things are based in immovable fact or are based around limiting beliefs you are holding.

For example, if you are overweight and you list out the things that are holding you back, it may look like this:

- I don't have enough time to eat well
- I can't afford to eat well
- I come from a fat family, so it's a genetic problem that I can't change
- I don't eat that much
- I don't snack that much

Things that hold me back:

time and resources on regularly unblocking, resolving, and blasting unhealthy beliefs and getting your mind free from negative programs. This will change your world and make you more healthy, successful, and happy instantly. We'll look at how you can do this in more detail later.

B. Blast out the spoilers
Doing a professional decluttering job for your mind is essential for everyone on a regular basis. We would never dream of leaving our houses without a sort out or a regular cleaning; yet, we let our minds continue on with some mad, bad, and dangerous-to-know programs that we have collected through the years. We allow them to remain, in many cases causing a complete mess and even decay in certain areas of our lives. We can see evidence of this all around us. We see certain friends going from one bad relationship to another. We watch others consistently losing jobs or getting into fights or being harassed by others. I know one famous person, for example, who picks fights so often with others that he regularly spends hundreds of thousands of dollars every year on lawsuits and legal bills for all the fighting he has to do; each year the same problems arise

Hold a still place within, close your eyes, go inside, and really pull out the things that you believe around the problem. Work with a friend to help you or, better still, use a professional coach to work through the beliefs, blast them out, and replace them with more constructive and useful ones. Beliefs are structured around emotions and definitions of what you believe to be true. Often there will be some false accounting and assumptions at work. Unblocking these will be your fastest route to joy and will strengthen your ability to manifest effectively.

Updating your mind software is something worth doing at least as often as you upgrade your computer's software. Spend some

Notes:

....

....

....

but with different people and in new guises. It is likely that this person has an unhelpful fight program running, rather than a lot of the same sort of bad luck occurring year after year.

Insist on a mind cleanse, a defragmentation of your mental hard drive and a spring cleaning for new ways of doing things with some new shiny belief systems which catapult you into the success stratosphere.

One great way to do this quickly is to get some one-on-one private sessions with a qualified practitioner to release your old negative programming.

C. Brain waves

There are different brain wave frequencies and some of these are more dynamic, powerful, and effective states for manifesting. In certain brain wave frequencies, we get access to something similar to a direct bridge to the place where experience and reality is formed. These are the desired brain states to create the most powerful place for manifesting and it is worth spending time defocusing to reach them.

How do we enter an ideal brain wave state for manifesting? By getting relaxed and going deep inside.

Here is a step-by-step guide for taking your mind into an altered, relaxed state, one which is going to help you make powerful intention and manifesting commands. Listen to the accompanying audio. Make sure that you are sitting comfortably in a relaxed place without distraction. Do not do this while driving.

Free your mind

01. Close your eyes and breathe deeply. For several minutes, allow your whole body to relax and allow thoughts to come in and float off without engaging in them. Just observe them and allow them to float away in the same way that you may notice clouds going by. Follow your breathing and notice it ebb and flow, in and out.

02. Bring your awareness to the center of your forehead, behind your third eye area, and allow your awareness to lift through the top of your head and into an imaginary elevator. Now, allow this elevator to go up and up and up and up, rising through many floors. Keep going up and you may allow your eyelids to flutter gently if you want.

Notes:

....

....

....

Keep floating up above the sky
and clouds, and reach an elevated
space. Let your mind go free.

Keep allowing any thoughts just
to float on by. Be an observer.
Do not engage in your thoughts—
just watch them.

Audio 07:

**This audio will get you feeling
relaxed and guide you into
expanding your viewpoint—
getting you into a great place
for manifesting.**

Audio

default personality. We can re create
who we are any time, so do so today
and choose a new version of you
loaded with success and happiness,
or whatever you choose, added
into the mix. This version can be as
exciting and as dynamic as you dare
to dream up. Make sure you access
the good feelings that correspond
with the version of you that you are
choosing. For example, if you choose
to be wealthy, make sure that you
pull in the feelings of already being
wealthy. Remember a time when
you felt wealthy or imagine that you
already are, then pull in all of these
feelings and have them fill your body.

D. Appreciation

Offering deep appreciation for what
you already have in your life will help.
It will rebalance and bring in some
positive frames over negative ones
to get you noticing what is going
well. Remember to bring in daily
appreciation for all aspects of life.
Write a list daily of everything
you are grateful for and appreciate.
This alone will bring radical and
positive change into your life fast.

E. Mind makeover

While you are doing a mind makeover
on yourself, remember to choose a
new version of you to install as your

Already having the feelings of the
thing you are choosing to create
is a key step to making the manifest
apparent. The visualization audios
that go with this book talk you
through how to do this.

F. Ego at work

Ego has an important role in our inner
world. **One of ego's jobs is to keep
us safe and on familiar ground,**
never far from where we know is safe.

Ego does a good job of keeping us
in our familiar zone and regular box
"away from trouble" (as the ego sees
it). The ego is powerful and well-

Notes:
....
....
....

equipped, with plenty of clever tricks to make sure that it does the best job possible by stopping any significant changes or personal expansion.

To manifest successfully and bring about positive changes, we need to take account of the fact that the ego will be working hard and doing everything in its power to prevent us from making any meaningful changes at all—good or bad. It does not judge what is good or bad for us; that is not the job of the ego. It is all about keeping things the same. More of the same equals "safe" in the realm of the ego.

For example, it is ego that will kick in to stop us pursuing the practice of conscious deliberating. It will encourage us to forget to do the techniques that will create changes in our life. It will come up with excuses, obstacles, and reasons for not taking action and will set up strong roadblocks to prevent us from changing our circumstances. **The ego resists us making changes.**

The good news is that there are ways around this. The first step in dealing with ego battle tactics is to notice that ego is trying hard to play tricks on us that will stop us changing. By becoming aware of this, we can take the necessary action and avoid the pitfalls by knowing about them ahead of time.

Ego may be tamed by understanding and awareness. By working with the ego and not against it you can harness its power and strength for your own purpose. The ego ultimately wants to help you and is a powerhouse of potentiality. By being clear in your own mind about where you are going in your life and who you are choosing to be, you can get the ego working with you and coming along for the ride.

Be aware that if the ego is working against you, it will create endless obstacles to getting things done. It will create blocks; it will create amnesia, causing you to forget to do the change work or it may blast you with negative mind chatter which can successfully destroy all the good work.

Ego is your own *self-image*; it is the social face of who you are in the world and it is the underlay in the roles you play in your life. It thrives on your public face; it wants to have its control and it wants to be a powerful force. This is in contrast to your *true*

Notes:

....

....

....

YES!

self, which is at ease and sits within the laws of nature effortlessly. The true self is being provided for by the support and the power of the universe. Your true self is gentler and understands that it is outside of ego.

An illusion of the ego is that it can easily feel that it is "you," when it is simply only a part of you that is operating in this way.

Hearing the voice of the ego from inside, while it instructs you to act in particular patterns, can cause major confusion and hold you back. However, if you are aware of this, then you are on the best path to avoid this pitfall. It is easy then to refer to the stronger yet quieter inner voice within, which is your real connective chord to your intuition and your pathway of truth.

There are exercises in Part C of this book which will allow you to successfully satisfy ego aspects so that it can integrate brilliantly into the new version of who you are choosing to be.

G. YES to all requests
What follows now is one of the most important pieces of information contained in this book.

The universal energy and the big picture of "all that is" has a keen need to please and is configured to give a resounding "yes" to all things asked.

The universe we inhabit always says "**yes**" to any request we make.

This is a rather important fact.

The universe says yes to every request that we make. When we ask for something in life, it is given to us precisely and exactly as we have asked for it.

Now this is all well and good providing that we are thinking and choosing what it is we do want in life. Sadly, we haven't been taught to always construct in terms of what we want. When we were young, we were probably not taught this. It is more likely that we were shown how to highlight what is not required and what is not working well by our major role models (parents/teachers).

Make sure that everything you instruct from within through your mind is always placed in positive terms. Your brain will ignore a negative construction and will simply take this as the thing you are asking for, so be very careful about how you frame

Notes:

....

....

....

the request. For example, framing for love in your life would be "I am choosing love in my life." If you were to request "I don't want to be lonely anymore," the universe would take this as an instruction about loneliness and would go ahead creating more aspects of loneliness to correspond with the lonely frequency and vibration being emitted.

Keep things stated in the positive and precisely how you want to bring them about.

Positive words:

H. Mind chat

We all have the soundtrack of "chatter" in our minds as we talk to ourselves within. It is important to pay attention to this aspect of mind chat and find out how you talk to yourself, so that you can correct it if necessary.

Many of us have developed negative mind chat and bad ways of talking to ourselves. We tell ourselves off, dwell on things that we don't want, look at the negative, or entertain mind chat about the bad things that are going on to prove to ourselves how bad life really is right now, and so on.

So, speaking to your inner self in a good way and engaging in encouraging positive and friendly internal mind chat is necessary for manifesting well. Pay close attention to that which you are saying inside your mind and make sure that it is positive and encouraging and based around what you're choosing to bring into your life consciously.

Many people do not know how they speak to themselves until they turn inside, tune in, and start listening for the very first time in many cases.

Let's try this out now.

Notes:

....

....

....

There is really no point in beating yourself up with harsh words on the inside. This is the quickest way to manifest badly and bring negative aspects into your life. So stop the bad voice immediately and **start talking to yourself nicely.**

Inner chat checker

01. How is the talk inside your head sounding to you now?

Just sit quietly and listen to your inner voice. Listen and notice what is being said within your own mind space.

Check the tone, for example is it:

Encouraging/polite/kind/warm/soothing/gentle

Strong/positive/comforting/pleasant

Nasty/aggressive/shouting/abrasive/unpleasant

Make a note here of how your inner talk sounds most of the time right now:

....

....

....

....

Check the content, for example is it:

Positive/encouraging/supportive/forgiving **or** abusive/negative/unsupportive/judging

Make a note here of the general content of your inner talk most of the time:

....

....

....

....

02. Would you date this voice?

Yes ☐   No ☐

Make a new choice concerning the voice you are going to use from now on for your inner talk. You get to decide what it sounds like in terms of the tone and the content. You may decide to make it soft and warm in tone, and encouraging and supportive in content. Make a new choice now and write it below.

Keep your inner talk in check. Monitor it regularly to support this new choice for your inner chat.

03. I am going to change my inner voice now to:

(tone) .... and

(content) ....

Now practice re-creating your voice inside your head, make it pleasant and kind and decide that from now on this voice will talk to you only in a positive and supportive way.

Instructions for positive mental mind chat

 Target

01. Make your inner voice sound soothing, kind, pleasant, and upbeat.

02. Make sure that the content of your mind chatter is positive and supportive and focused around what you are intending from now on.

03. Make a decision now to banish negativity from your mind chat forever.

04. Start now by exercising new, positive mind chat. Begin by asking your voice inside to tell you five things that you love about yourself, how great you are, and what a wonderful human being you are. Do this while looking in the mirror for a bit of extra potency.

How much resistance did you have to doing this? If this is easy for you, full marks. The process will be straightforward and easy. If this is hard for you, then take notice that you need to pay close attention to upgrading your inner talk immediately and decide to do this 100% of the time from now on.

Whenever you catch yourself speaking badly inside your mind, just know that you can change the tone, the content, and the intention of the soundtrack being played and switch it to a friendlier, kinder sound. Like all mind methods, this is easy, as long as you actually remember to do it.

Remember to do it and make a point of doing it. Write reminder notes around your house and use the technique consciously.

Changing your inner voice sound track to a better one will change your life immediately in the most amazing way. It will be one of the most revolutionary things you have done to jump-start a happier life and expand into a better experience.

I. Mind map
The power of your imagination in creating reality follows these rules whether you believe it or not. It really doesn't matter whether you believe any of this is true; it will continue to work anyway.

Therefore, if you are interested in shaping the outcome of your own life to one of wonder, happiness, and joy, then use these tools and do not worry whether they are true,

Notes:
....
....
....

or whether you believe them or not, as this is not going to be relevant to the success of the outcome. Use the techniques and, further down the line, you can sort out your own belief systems on it all if you want to.

We are only interested here in learning the tools for creating and manifesting a wonderful life. It is not the intention of this book to impart any specific beliefs or understandings about how the world works as being definitive or absolute truths. We are using models for mind mapping happiness and success—and they are very effective too.

Just as you would read a manual to find out how to get the best power out of your latest gadget, this book gives you a map for mind success and expanding your life. You don't have to understand or believe how electricity works to know that when you press the computer power on, your computer will start up and perform very useful activities for you.

You do not need to understand fully how everything works, or even believe that it works in the way that it does; you just need to be able to operate your mind in the best way to get the best out of it.

Fold out to reveal your mind map
for happiness and success …

Mind map ...

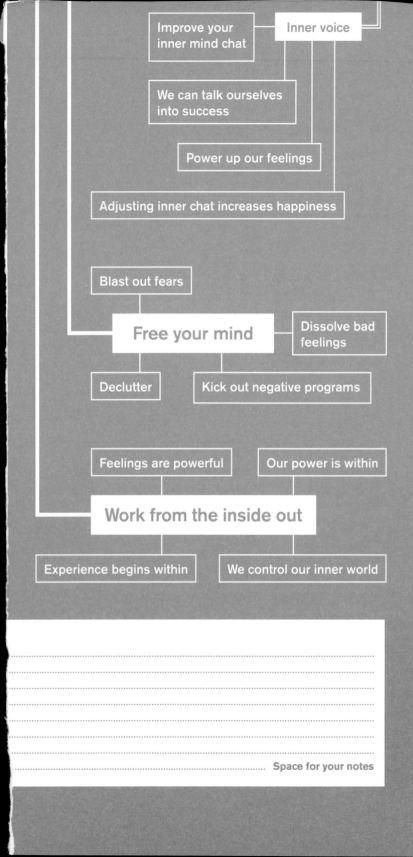

Improve your inner mind chat

Inner voice

We can talk ourselves into success

Power up our feelings

Adjusting inner chat increases happiness

Blast out fears

Free your mind

Dissolve bad feelings

Declutter

Kick out negative programs

Feelings are powerful

Our power is within

Work from the inside out

Experience begins within

We control our inner world

Space for your notes

We choose how we respond to every event in life

We decide our state

Create strong states

Positive states make us more successful

Being happy and successful is a choice

Frame all things in the positive

Ask for what you want

Be positive

The universe says yes to all requests

We attract what we think about

Thoughts are creative

Thoughts are powerful

Be disciplined about the contents of your thoughts

Align with the version you choose to be

Align

Get the feelings of having the life you choose

For hap
and suc

My mind map ...

Charting out ideas in a mind map gets your mind focused and energized to start creating your plans.

Begin by drawing your own mind map here and outlining key ideas that you would like to activate and create in your life. There are no rules (except have fun and no holding back).

Starting point:

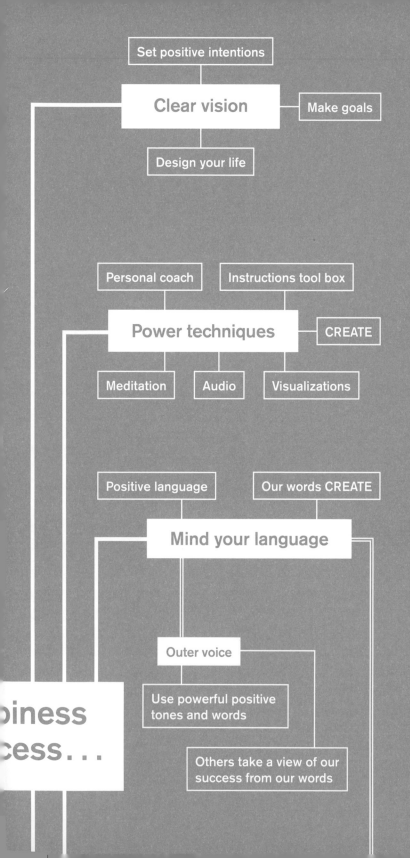

Be aware of ego's dirty tricks to hold you back

Your ego may not want you to change

Ego tricks

Run your own mind—take control

Get more aware of what you think, feel, and say

Mind makeover

Feel better first then let life catch up

Say "thank you"

Push up gratitude

Appreciation

Notice what you've already got

Be it. . .

Free your mind and everything is possible.

Chapter 9 checklist	☑
Upgrade your mental software	☐
Identify and blast limiting beliefs out of your mind	☐
Hire a mentor to help clear negative programs	☐
Bathe yourself in gratitude and appreciation	☐
Choose a new version of you	☐
Get the feeling	☐
Beware of ego tricks	☐
The universe says YES to all requests	☐
Clear negative mind chatter	☐
Follow and apply your own mind map for success	☐
Expand your life	☐
Free your mind and everything is possible	☐

Notes:

....

....

....

The tool kit:

In Part C we apply what we have learned in Parts A and B. Here you will find tools that give you practical methods of making the knowledge work in your life today in ways that will create great changes, fast improvements, and bring you closer to abundance, wealth, and happiness than you have ever experienced before. This tool kit provides you with proven techniques to bring in the things you are looking to activate in your life. Use them at any time, in any order, and use them regularly. You may notice the results coming in ways that will amaze you. Prepare for the unexpected.

Part

C

Tools

Time to play and have some fun.

Tool kit for success

Do you want more wealth, health, happiness, success, life direction, and financial abundance in your life? If so, read on, as this is the section that will transform these areas fast.

This tool kit is organized to be used randomly. You can mix and match these exercises in ways to focus and activate specific areas at any time depending upon what you want to create. If you work on tools that energize general abundance, you may find all areas of your life transforming together. You can use the tools in any order and mix them up successfully. There is no way that you can overdo the work, however be careful not to create "push" or "needy" energy with your intentions. Be easy with it all and give it a light as a feather touch with

Notes:
....
....
....

your mind work. Relax, have faith, and allow it to come to you gently and in a matter-of-fact way. Don't feel rushed on time—the time will be when it will be.

You may well find that things start to change and come in quite fast. Sometimes it may feel like life is becoming quite dynamic, choppy, topsy-turvy, or strained. In this case, simply acknowledge and see that this is a case of some turmoil created in order to bring change and new structures in your life to reflect what you are calling in. For example, to clean up a closet, you may need to empty it all out first, make a mess, then throw some things away, and repack the rest in a way that looks much better, and is much more organized and pleasing. It is the same with life: sometimes it's a mess, throwing out and chaos needs to happen in order to learn, find, what you do want, and get your life in order and restructured in a way that makes you happy and harmonious.

Following your work on positive beliefs and new thinking, welcome any big changes, knowing that they will be serving you well and that you are on the road to the best changes for your highest and greatest good.

Sometimes we resist change but, in fact, this is often the very thing that we need to embrace to get our life on track. If you can see everything coming into your life as ultimately perfect (even if you can't see the big picture quite at this moment), then this will help you to see these elements as important lessons and allow the necessary shifts to happen with grace so that everything you have asked for is delivered to you swiftly. It is law: you ask, you allow with faith and gratitude, you receive. This happens 100% of the time. No exceptions.

The exercises in this tool kit are designed to get you to spend more time focusing directly on what you choose, to become more aware of your feelings and emotions, and to let these guide you to get on track. You will learn to build stronger internal states and to activate and positively manage your inner manifesting skills. We need to know and to remember how to use them effectively if we are to lead abundant and successful lives. We can all do this—it depends upon how well we understand the Law of Attraction and how well we are managing our internal state and focus.

Notes:

....

....

....

Stay on focus—stay positive—keep centered—hold your vibration steady —know the creation rules

 Target

These activities are designed to steer you away from the negative, away from bad self-talk, and away from engaging in downbeat stories about your life. Instead, they encourage you to think and focus on what you choose, to create good positive emotions, and to hold your emotions steady without being influenced by things going on around you. You cannot control others and others cannot control you. No one has the power to control how you feel—only you have this power.

Life rules for happiness

01. You are what you think; your thoughts are energy and are magnetic. You attract directly into your life through your own thoughts and emotions. Like attracts like in all cases. For example, giving out love attracts love back to you and giving out hate attracts hate back to you.

02. You create everything that shows up in your life, so only you are the master of life's outcomes.

03. You can make changes to your life immediately—by changing your thoughts and feelings to focus positively on what you want and taking your attention away from what you don't.

04. Others cannot affect your outcome and you are not entitled to influence the outcome of others—only your own. Each person has free will and this must be respected.

05. We are emotional beings constantly transmitting magnetic frequencies. These frequencies attract a magnetic match of circumstance and events toward us.

06. All requests you make through word, thought, feelings, wishes, or prayers are answered by the universe, 100% of the time, no exceptions. The universe always says yes and will deliver.

07. You can be, have, do anything you choose—as long as you believe that you can and you let go of forcing the outcome.

08. Managing your own mind is the most powerful thing you can do to change your life, and it affects your whole being and life experience.

09. You do have the power to change your life dramatically in any way you choose and you are doing this every moment.

10. Your vibrational set point at any time affects how much of the good stuff comes your way.

11. The universe does not judge whether what you are asking for is "good" or "bad." It does not pull back if it seems that you made a lousy choice; it simply reflects your choices, whether "positive" or "negative." Your life experience tells you exactly how well you are doing in your choices and asking.

12. Avoid negative thoughts, mind chatter, words, and emotions.

13. Avoid negativity in your environment, such as toxic people, gossip, conversations, negative news, and clutter.

14. Tell a new story of how you are choosing things to be (you do not have to tell it as it is right now).

15. As it is right now is a result of previous thinking.

16. There is a lead time between setting up your new manifesting choices and experiencing them; this is in the design of nature and helps to prevent chaos and the calling in of fifty-thousand items daily, randomly, and chaotically.

17. You choose your partners, your friends, your luck, and every outcome you experience. The responsibility for your own life's unfolding is 100% with you. No one else is to blame for any aspect of your experience. You made it all.

18. You are what you think, eat, and vibrate, as well as being your environment, so choose well. You choosing something in your life does not stop another from having it. This is a kindly universe of abundance with infinite energy resources.

19. Education, social strata, job, or circumstances do not prevent you from choosing or having whatever you want in life.

20. Quiet, still time is essential for high-end success. The most successful people maintain a peaceful mind space, quiet time, and harmony to create from and through which they power up their successful mind states. Meditation, quiet reflection, a state of harmony, and peace are essential for success.

21. Other aspects of successful manifesting include desire, clarity, harmony, cooperation, a frame of love, a focus on the good, bringing together other great harmonious minds, faith, and understanding that you are creating it all and have the power to create anything.

Tool 01: CREATE box

We are going to begin with one of my favorite techniques. This is the one which has time after time provided astonishing results for many of my clients and often on a much greater scale than was originally asked for.

Method
01. Gather a beautiful looking box. You can use an attractive gift box, a colorful document box, or make something yourself. Make sure it looks lush and attractive. Write out the following statement and put it on top of the box as a label:

> Whatever is contained in this box I have already created in my mind and welcome into my life now. Everything in this box is already present. I receive all of this with abundance and flow.
>
> All for the best.
>
> Thank you. It's done. Show me.

02. Gather together pictures and items to visualize your wishes and intentions, i.e., what you are asking to

Notes:
....
....
....

create. Collect visuals which evoke a good feeling and clarify precisely what you are wishing for. These may be from brochures, magazines, pictures downloaded from the Web, hand-drawn pictures, written words on a piece of beautiful paper—anything that clearly and precisely describes your desires. You may be looking to visualize a beautiful relationship, a career promotion, improved health, a car, a new outfit, a dream date, a new home overlooking some water, an improved job opportunity, exam success, or an unexpected windfall. Of course, you can choose anything you like.

These are just a few ideas to get you started.

Choose things to begin with that you can easily imagine creating in your life.

Gather together your materials and place each of them into your box one by one while being in a positive mental state and thinking to yourself or stating out loud the following:

"I am ready to allow this to flow into my life right now. I have faith, excitement, and the feelings of having this or something better.

Thank you. It's already done. Show me."

03. Now, place the item into the box with the feeling of excitement of already having this in your life. Keep doing this with all of the things that you are choosing to bring in. Then close the lid, feel it is already done, and continue with your day. Walk and breathe like these things are already in your life. Feel like you have this with you. Imagine it being already here.

04. Revisit the box regularly and review your items. Keep an eye on them, keep them in your mind, think about them often, as if you already have them with you; be careful not to focus on the thought of them not being here yet, as this will create the opposite effect and a "lack" vibration. You can change the items whenever you wish. Keep consistency as much as possible so that the same instruction gets transmitted out clearly and powerfully.

Outcome
This is a powerful instruction generator and clarifier of what you are choosing to create. It pays back with an incredible success rate. I have hundreds of examples

Notes:

....

....

....

of extraordinary serendipity from my clients who have successfully activated reality creation through using this CREATE box technique. Try it today. It works like a dream.

Something magical happens with this process. For example, when I first tried this process, I got my box ready and put into it a photo of a picturesque country house from a magazine. The picture showed a beautiful house with white wood timbers on one side, a beautiful mosaic swimming pool, a weeping willow over the edge of a tennis court, wonderful paddock lands with a pond, and timber beams running through the living room which had unusual large black printed letters and numbers running along the sides. I had no idea where this place was but I knew I liked the look and the feel of it and would love to live somewhere like this sometime in my life. At the time, I lived in a pleasant townhouse in London with a manageable yard—nothing like this country pile. We had not discussed plans to leave the city and we had not considered a move to the country. The following week, we were given notice that we had to leave our house in London and move out unexpectedly. I was shocked and pretty upset. I had grown used to our house and loved where we were overlooking the River Thames in London.

Within eight short weeks, we had moved into a place in a beautiful quiet country village in Kent, England. It was a magnificent house with white timbers on one side, a pool and terrace, a tennis court with a weeping willow tree at the side, a well-stocked pond, and all of the elements that were in the picture resting in my CREATE box. Most intriguingly, there were beams running through the open plan living room with large black numbers and letters running across—just like the photograph in my box. The house had been a working Oast House, where hops and beer were made many years ago. The inscriptions on the wooden beams indicated which hops and grains were being stored from which year so that the brewers would know which harvest they were working with. I knew then beyond any doubt that the CREATE box works. I couldn't believe it and this gave me proof beyond all proof—this works and it works fast.

Some years later, I put a magazine picture of another house in my

Notes:

....

....

....

CREATE box. This time it was a big white house, with a red-walled ballroom with parquet flooring, and a maze in the yard. We moved into an identical looking home within three months. In my new yard was a maze. It is so similar in style that I show these pictures at seminars to students to show the extraordinary similarity of what went in the box, and what arrived in reality a short time later.

I told my friend Paul McKenna about this extraordinary success tool. He tried it out immediately and was amazed at the power of the manifesting speed. It worked for him too. Then I heard the same story from many of my clients: magnificent success with this technique beyond all expectations.

It has not let me down. I use it regularly as a great tool to focus and create fast, accurate manifestations. Years later, I still have my box close by my side and use it all the time for building successful manifesting creations.

Tool 02: The GGRR journal

This daily journal to express gratitude, giving, receiving, and rejoicing will get you into the state of appreciation—a prime state for creating an amazing magnetic pull to bring positive aspects into your life in all areas. This is the state that you need to be in to manifest strongly and to create great things fast.

The advantage of doing this exercise regularly is that it will put you in the right state of vibration for manifesting—perfectly primed to receive wonderful things into your life.

Method
Keep a daily GGRR journal.

01. Select a new notebook and allocate a page a day for your notes. Divide the page into four areas with these headings: Gratitude, Giving, Receiving, Rejoicing. Note the following in each section:

Gratitude: Everything you are grateful for this day.

Giving: Everything that you have given joyfully on this day.

Receiving: Everything that you gratefully received on this day.

Rejoicing: Everything that you are rejoicing about in your life today.

Note: The items to notice are often

Notes:
....
....
....

life's simple things: a kind look from a stranger, a warm smile from a friend, wonderful food, going for a walk with a pet or loved one, noticing a change in the seasons, the first signs of sunshine, freshness of rain, and so on. Of course, you can include the obvious great things in life too—a promotion, a hug, a new purchase, or receiving an unexpected or expected payment of some kind.

02. The best time to do your journal is either first thing in the morning (within fifteen minutes of waking) or last thing at night (fifteen minutes before sleeping). If you do it at the start of the day, you can write it as if you are choosing and imagining how your day will turn out ahead of time.

If you are doing it at the end of the day, then it becomes a review of the day. It doesn't need to take long. Five minutes or so is fine. It is important that you do this regularly and make it part of your daily routine, and you'll see amazing results.

Outcome

One of the best techniques around for keeping you in a space and attitude of gratitude and appreciation for what you already have in your life. This position is an absolute

requirement in order to be a powerful and positive manifestor. Keeping a GGRR journal will transform your life. I have known people to have extraordinary transformations fast just by doing this one exercise.

Tool 03: Pump up the money

This is a great tool for creating more money in your life. There are quite a few people who could do with a bit of this. Follow the guide below for increasing cash flow into your life easily.

Method

01. Get a check book (or make up an imaginary one from some paper cut to size) and write yourself a check for CASH to the tune of fifty dollars or whatever your currency. Now think for a moment how you will spend this money and write it down exactly in a notebook until all the money is "spent" each day in full. You must "spend it" in your journal; you are not allowed to hoard it.

02. The next day, do the same again but this time double the amount. You must "spend" it all and write down in full what you are spending your imagined cash on. It's all

Notes:

....

....

....

Tools

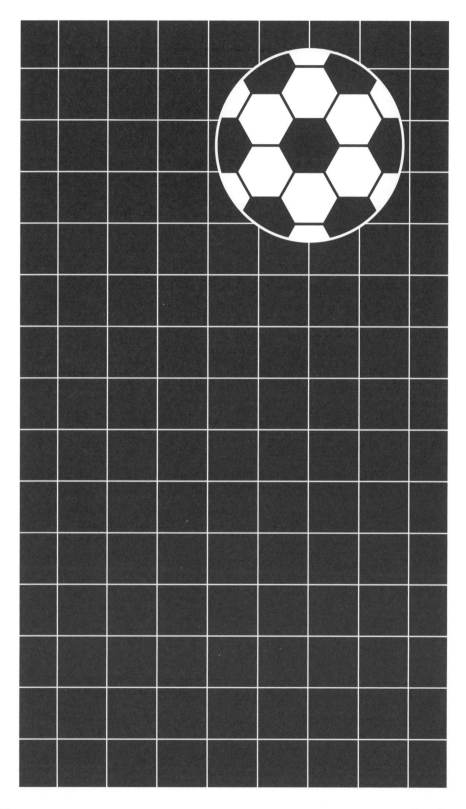

imagined, so go to town with your creative thinking. It can be as ludicrous and as far-fetched as you like, as long as the purchase makes you feel good, happy, and excited.

03. Each day, double the amount and write down how you are imagining spending it.

04. Feel the feelings of actually spending this money and keep a log of everything you have bought with this money. Do this every day for at least a month. Have fun with it.

Outcome

Your wealth barometer will soar very quickly. Your mind—which does not know the difference between imagined and real—will be sending out clear messages to your "being" state that you have plenty of cash and are spending happily, daily, and in increasing amounts. This will increase your internal wealth barometer fast which in turn will magnetically attract more wealth into your life and into your reality.

This works like a dream by the way—I have road tested it successfully and many of my clients have too. One client was imagining purchasing power boats and villas in Tuscany for this exercise and is now doing this for real in life; it all panned out as imagined and ricocheted into reality fast. It will for you as well if you do it with focus, intent, confidence, and excitement.

Tool 04: Goal setter

This is shocking but true: When clients start work with me, over 90% of them do not have a clear idea about their personal goals, aspirations, visions, or what they want to achieve. When asked, most people do not know their dreams. Unless you know where you want to go, you have no hope of getting there.

Set out to make some clear goals today, get clarity on this area, and write it all down. You cannot hope for success by manifesting well if you have not been clear about intention-setting.

Write whatever springs into your mind, do this quickly and without too much thought. Just write down your first answers. You can go back, amend, and update this list anytime. Remember to keep it private or just between you and a professional mentor if you have one.

Notes:

....

....

....

Method

01. Write down your life goals for different time spans.

My life goals for the next ...

... week: ....
....
....
....

... month: ....
....
....
....

... six months: ....
....
....
....

... one year: ....
....
....
....

... five years: ....
....
....
....

... ten years: ....
....
....

Goal setter...

Tool 04.
Work out what you want
and where you're going.

Other:

....
....
....
....
....
....
....

03. Revisit your visions and goals often and refine them. Is this worth the investment of fifteen minutes of your time? Yes.

Outcome

By setting your goals, you are giving the universe a clear indication of what you want to manifest. Only by doing this clearly and writing it down can your manifesting begin to take shape and you can see your dreams come into reality. Connections and synchronicities will begin to come into your life and be activated. The universe is delivering to you exactly what you are asking for and it requires clear instructions. It cannot guess what you are after; you must state it yourself and have it clear in your own mind. I am always astonished about how few people have set out their goals and visions and then wonder why "things are just not working out" the way they want.

All the successful people I know have clear visions and goals. By having these, you will have clarity and you will activate the success button inside yourself.

02. Write down your goals for the different areas of your life:

Love:

....
....
....
....
....
....
....
....
....

Wealth:

....
....
....
....
....
....
....
....

Well-being:

....
....
....
....
....
....
....

Fun & leisure:

....
....
....
....
....
....
....

Career:

....
....
....
....
....
....

Personal fulfillment & education:

....
....
....
....
....
....

Adventure:

....
....
....
....
....
....

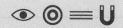

Tool 05: Review your life and make improvements

Do a quick review of your life as it is today.

Method

01. Get a blank piece of paper and divide it into four equal areas. Label these: **Strength, Weakness, Opportunity,** and **Threat**. Do an honest and full assessment of where your life is today for each of these headings.

02. In a different colored pen, make a note of any steps you can take to move yourself into a better place with each of these areas. For example:

Strong

I am a good dad/I have a sound family/I'm healthy/I have a lot of experience at work.

- get my family to contribute more to jobs around the house
- write a new CV
- stress less
- enjoy our family trips out more

Weak

I have debts/I'm not earning enough/I've got too much to do/I'm bored with my job/I'm overweight

- get a debt plan sorted out
- look for another way to earn extra money from home
- set up direct payments for bills to save time
- start fast walking five to ten minutes each lunchtime

Opportunity

I know there's a new job coming up at work/I could move home next year/I've met a friend who could help me find a new job at his work.

- make enquiries to the right person about the new job at work
- write a wish list for my next home
- speak to the person who can help me find a new job in the next three days

Threat

I may lose my job, house bills looming, and feel stressed all the time

- start looking for other options
- call the utility companies and ask to set up a payment plan
- relax more
- go swimming to get more energy
- get more sleep
- change my stress focus to a better feeling whenever I feel anxious

Notes:

....

....

....

Tool 06: The book of requests

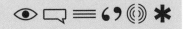

Outcome

Many of us rarely take a snapshot of our life and look at it objectively to see what we can easily do to make things better.

By doing a review, we can instantly see the major areas that are good and not good, and thereby make some informed choices for changing things around to make improvements.

By thinking about a few steps to take you into a better place in each of these areas, you will be taking control of your life and this will make you feel better. If you go forward, improving your life areas one step at a time, then you will feel that you are heading along a better road in life.

Tool 06: The book of requests

The legend of Aladdin's lamp is one of the most famous stories from *The Arabian Nights*. In the story, a genie emerges when the old dusty lamp is rubbed and grants the master of the lamp three wishes. The genie says, "Master, your wish is my command" and the wishes are granted without question and without alteration.

In a way, this is precisely what you have available to you through the

Laws of Manifesting and by directing your thoughts and feelings—you are able to ask the universal genie with certainty and clarity and know that you will receive your wishes. To sharpen up the creation process, I have found that creating and regularly using a book of requests is very useful indeed and provides astounding results.

Method

01. Find yourself a beautiful book with empty pages and use this to write your list of up to *three requests to the universe*. Include with these instructions your thanks for already having granted these requests.

You can visualize your requests using pictures and images as well as words and sentences to commit your requests to the page.

For example:

> Dear Universe,
>
> Please grant me the following three requests. Thank you:
>
> **1.** A promotion at work in the next three months. **2.** A new partner who I love and loves me. **3.** A resolution of my issues with Lisa at work, so I can move on learning what I need to learn from it, so that something similar is not repeated.
>
> It's done. Thank you. Show me.

Notes:

....

....

....

02. Once done, and as you shut the book, know that your instruction has already been sent off to the universal machine and the thing is in process. Consider it done, just like rubbing the Aladdin's lamp and knowing your three wishes are granted. They will be.

03. Rest in the feeling of already having these things present, have faith about this, and continue on with your day—with a smile and good feelings running through your body.

04. Run this process as many times as you like. I recommend up to five times daily. Repeat and review your wishes regularly.

Outcome

This tool will help you form focused, clear intentions sent out as clear instructions to the universal machine.

Set, aim, and fire. Result.

Tool 07: Payday plan

Are you feeling stress over bills you have to pay every month? Here is a great tool for reducing any stress you might be feeling around your finances which will improve your financial vibrations.

Method

01. Allocate one afternoon a week (or every two weeks, or once a month) to handle your bills and get paperwork done. This means that there is a specific time you have to do this and the rest of the time you are completely free of it. Make a note of the day and time slot to do this in your diary and label it as "Payday" (this should have good connotations to you as it gives the feeling that you are the one getting paid).

02. When you receive a bill, take it and place it straight into an inbox or folder and put this out of sight into a cupboard or filing cabinet (unless it's urgent for immediate attention, of course).

03. At the appointed time slot in the diary, get out your inbox or folder and go through everything in there and deal with it. Touch each piece of paper only once, pay the bill (or better still, set up a scheduled direct debit to pay it automatically which will give you one less thing to do each time) and feel glad to be paying the bill.

Feel joyous and happy to be spending money and feel rich as you pay it, knowing that you can do

Notes:

....

....

....

it easily and it makes you feel good. Circulating money and allowing it to flow in and out easily is a fast track to being abundant. Bless the payment as you put it in the envelope or as you do the transfer online. After this, mark the bill clearly as PAID and then file it carefully into a well-organized ring binder with the other bills. Feel good that you have dealt with this and give it good energy.

Now forget about the bills and move on with something else.

04. If you have too many bills for your earnings, take stock. Go through all of your outgoings carefully, do a monthly budget sheet of incoming and outgoing, and see where you are. If things are out of hand, then look to set up a Debt Management Plan or an arrangement with each supplier and have an agreement in place; then pay it this way and forget about it the rest of the time. Focus now on building your money up and earning more and more funds easily and effortlessly rather than having a debt focus. Put your focus on the aspect of building your pot and increasing your wealth each day. Take your focus completely off debts except for the nominated time slot you have allocated to deal with them.

If there is something that needs urgent attention, then mark in your diary to deal with it in an appropriate amount of time so there isn't undue stress. You'll find that money management is easier to handle and not on your mind all the time. If the bills are out of sight for the most part, then your mind can focus on more profitable areas, like wealth creation.

Deal with things early and head-on with a plan and a solution-based frame. You will feel so much better having it all dealt with. It will be a stress literally out of sight.

Outcome
Looking at bills and debts every day will keep you in the frequency of being in lack and debt and this will keep you in a downbeat place financially. You will simply attract more lack and more debt. By allocating yourself a specific time in the week or month to deal with bills, you will be taking control of your focus and giving yourself the best chance of staying in a good healthy vibration with your money management and saying goodbye to debt consciousness forever.

This will radically change your financial outlook.

Notes:

....

....

....

Tool 08: Pay yourself first

Tool 08: Pay yourself first

Here are the three great pieces of advice regarding money flow:

i. Set your internal wealth barometer to a high setting

ii. Save 10% or more of your earnings each month regularly

iii. Pay yourself first

They are all simple, magnificent principles and work like a dream.

Method

01. Close your eyes and imagine that you have an inner "wealth barometer." Imagine that it measures how much wealth you allow in to your life. Set this gauge now to a new level of your choice. It can be set to fair, good, very good, or excellent; it's your choice and will determine how you do in your life financially.

02. Save at least 10% of everything that you earn, right from the start, in a savings plan every month. This 10% goes straight into your savings account and does not get spent.

03. As soon as you get paid, pay yourself first. This may be anything from 5% or more of your total earnings. This payment is separate to your savings amount. You become the priority creditor on your list of payments each month.

How you do this: First, work out a budget based on how much you earn and what your fixed expenses are each month. Set it all out clearly and see what is left (if anything). If you have an amount left over as available, then nominate an affordable sum to pay yourself each month for your **fun fund**.

You can then use this amount in any way you choose—leisure, towards vacations or a new car, general fun, and going out. Make sure that you get paid first, as a matter of priority, and then use this money happily to have some fun. That way, you always have money to play with each month.

Note that you must have done a proper living expenses budget and be clear on all of your outgoings and likely incomings to do this effectively and for it to work properly. It all hinges on having a clear picture of your finances. Divide your money up in a way that makes the most sense and allows you some spare spending money each month. Taking control of money begins by knowing how much

Notes:

....

....

....

you have to work with and go from there with a plan and a strategy for growing your wealth.

In addition, you can choose to segment your weekly/monthly/yearly income which will give you more control over your finances and more freedom. An example:

Split up your earnings and put it into separate accounts for:

- **55%** expenses/costs (home, car, food, etc.)
- **10%** to save
- **10%** to invest
- **10%** to play
- **10%** to learn
- **5%** to give away

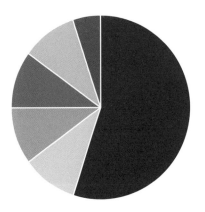

With this method, you know exactly how much you have to spend in each category and you will have clear funds in nominated categories to save, to give away, and to play. This creates balance and harmony with your finances and helps you build a strong base and more secure future.

Outcome
Completing this simple exercise will create sound financial management, peace, a savings plan that can build fast, and a sense of being in control of your financial resources.

Whether you are feeling wealthy or not right now, this will put anyone into a great position financially.

Tool 09: Walking in gold dust

In the 1980s, I founded a hugely successful PR agency which won high-profile and prestigious projects right from the start. We were working early on with big names such as Sony, Microsoft, MTV, and Madonna. The company is still going strong. It has grown to be one of the top entertainment and brand agencies in the world. What was the secret to our early and ongoing significant success?

Notes:

....

....

....

I was often asked this question by the press, clients, and friends. I usually made up an answer along the lines of following my gut intuition, always being honest in our dealings, over delivering on promises, providing a great service, being fun people to do business with, and so on.

None of these were the real-deal answer. No one would have believed me if I had told them the real reason behind our extraordinary success.

The secret weapon behind our success was a store of gold dust, which I pulled into play as required using my imagination. I knew how to bring it into any situation and how to use it when we needed some special help and a positive outcome for something important or that looked tricky. I used it in everyday situations as well as at major pitches, as it felt so good to use and always seemed to work.

This gold dust would help me create a successful outcome every time. I would use it secretly and liberally when we needed to win a pitch or do a stunning presentation for a new client or campaign. I used it to run successful meetings, create outcomes in phone calls that matched my intentions, and to win multi-million dollar pitches against other, bigger agencies in town, which had larger budgets than us and double the staff. It worked every time except twice. Both times that it "didn't work," it turned out that the clients in question went bust. We would have lost money had we taken on the work and so each instance was a blessing that worked directly in our favor after all, though I didn't realize this until later.

Method
01. When you need some extra special help from the universe or just to have a great day, imagine the following scene:

Walk as the successful version of you would walk. Stand tall, feel statuesque, and feel like you are looking particularly good and feel loaded with success. Now, imagine as you walk along that a huge sprinkling of sparkling gold dust is falling down on you from above, and as it does so, it brings with it magic and success so that everything turns out just as you wish. As you feel it fall on you, become aware of the feeling of having things turn out perfectly, of feeling lucky, of being guided to success, and having all of the

Notes:
....
....
....

resources of the universal machinery doing its stuff and bringing you the perfect solutions on time, in perfect harmony with everything else. Voila.

02. Alternatively, shower in a waterfall of imaginary gold dust each morning, and feel the power and success come down on you as you stand and enjoy your shower. Feel like you are bathing in luck. Visualize it, feel it and you are good to go for a happy, successful day.

Outcome
This exercise works wonders, and I can tell you that it has worked for me for two decades and allowed me to create one of the most successful entertainment PR agencies in the world while I was still very young. It has worked in extraordinary ways for everyone I have introduced it to. You will find success falls into your lap, things just appear that make everything turn out great and magnificence is yours. It also gives you an effervescent glow that others can sense and actually see.

When I do it, often people will say to me that I look glowing and indeed I am. There is magic behind this technique that is simply inexplicable and I invite you to try it.

Tool 09: Drop the donkey story

What story do you tell most often? We all have a regular default position for the kind of stories that we tell to express who we are and how we are living. Here are some examples:

Donkey storylines:

- Poor me: I've been taken advantage of again. Here's how it happened this time . . .

- Let me tell you all the things that went wrong for me today . . .

- Everyone loves to trip me up and it's happened again . . .

- Things are going wrong again . . .

- People at work don't like me . . .

- I hate people at work . . .

- What's wrong with him is . . .

- I don't have enough money to . . .

- I am always poor . . .

- I haven't got enough . . .

- I never have enough . . .

- I can't pay the bills . . .

- There is another bill to pay. I don't know what I am going to do . . .

- I'm worried sick about . . .

Notes:

....

....

....

Tell a better story.

- I am frightened that . . .

- I am terrified of . . .

- I am worried we can't make ends meet because . . .

- My wife doesn't understand me, here's why . . .

- My drama today is . . .

- It went wrong because . . .

- My life is a nightmare because . . .

- I feel ill . . .

- I feel miserable . . .

- I feel poor . . .

- I am unhappy because . . .

- I am really angry because . . .

- I am frustrated with . . .

- I am fed up with . . .

- Nothing is going right for me at the moment . . .

Or, you may be telling more of these sorts of stories.

Visionary storylines:

- Life is great because . . .

- I feel lucky because . . .

- I tried doing this and it went well . . .

- Here is what I did to make myself feel better today . . .

- My life is all about having fun and being in joy. This is what I am doing today to keep this coming in my life . . .

- I have plenty of money for the things I want.

- I love my work and my team.

- I really enjoy what I do.

- I love doing well and make a point of striving for this daily.

- I enjoy learning new things.

- I keep my mind on what I am feeling and head toward feeling good.

- If I ever start to feel bad, I find ways to change what I am doing so that I feel better.

- I had fun today.

- I tried something new and it worked.

- I love life.

- I am happy.

- I am grateful for everything I have.

- I feel rich in so many ways.

- I feel vibrant and strong.

- I am fit.

Notes:

....

....

....

- I eat well and rest well.

- My body is healthy and supports me wonderfully.

- I make a point of eating well and healthily every day.

- I look after myself.

- I love who I am. I love my family.

It will come as no surprise to learn that the first set of stories will lead to a stressful, negative existence. The second set of storylines, however, will lead you directly to being successful, having plenty, and living the life of your dreams.

Are you predominately telling the Donkey stories or the Visionary stories? It doesn't matter if you are saying these storylines in your head or out loud; either way, you are choosing as your focus to look at the bad parts or look at the good parts of life.

Whichever you are focusing on will create your dominant frequency and, by the Law of Attraction, more of the same will come right back at you.

You can have either outcome; it just depends upon which story style you choose to tell.

Method

01. When someone asks you, "How's things with you today?" Move towards answering this not by what you see in your life at this moment (a result of your past thinking). Instead, choose to answer this question from the positioning of "*How would you like it to be?*"

02. Speak about how you want to see your life patterning out. **Tell a better story.** Do not worry about it "not being true." You know the Law of Attraction, and if you want change, you have to be that change first and then it will show up. So telling it as you want it to be is simply the first step in successfully creating positive change in your life.

To the reply, "But it's not true," you could say: "It's not true yet. But that is how it will be for sure." Tell it the way you want it to be and align with it. Through the Law of Attraction, by focusing on this, you will indeed have it show up in your life in no time.

Outcome

Have a much better life when you tell a better story.

A miserable life will be yours if your story is downbeat.

Notes:
....
....
....

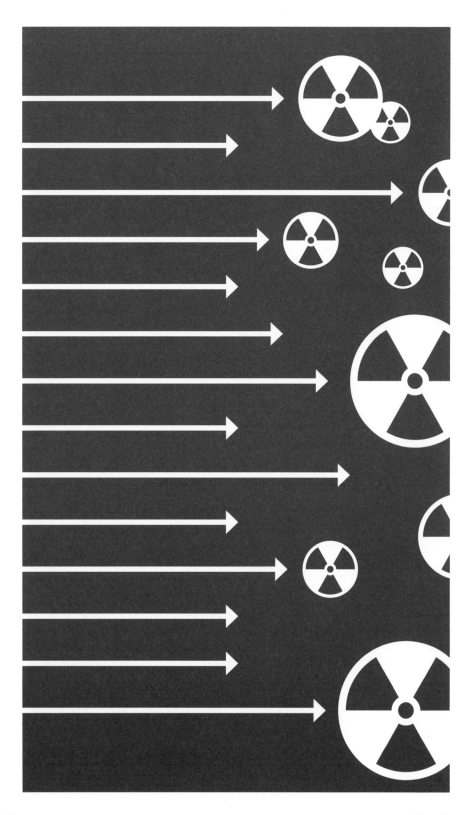

Tool 11: Toxic sweep

We all have toxicity in our lives to different degrees. The level of toxicity we allow in affects how successful and how happy we become moment by moment. Most of us would not dream of living in dirty homes which have never been cleaned up or from which no garbage has ever been discarded. Why should we treat our minds any differently?

It is time to commit to a regular detox of the mind: Clear away old belief patterns no longer serving you (changing from "I don't have enough money" to "I allow money into my life easily and regularly" for example), push up your moods and emotions to higher frequencies, and allow yourself to come from a place of non judgment and love. Look for the good and think better thoughts.

More than this, complete a toxic sweep of our environmental influences and the images that you take in. One of the most useful things you can do is stop watching the news which contains almost completely negative information: death, accidents, terrorism, bad economic forecasts, and terrible dramas. Why would we tune in to get more of this each day? It makes no sense at all, from a Law of Attraction perspective, to fill our minds with such low-vibration material.

Instead, read uplifting books, listen to some inspiring and happy music, exercise, go out in nature, or go and have a laugh with some uplifting friends. It is much better to raise your frequency and vibration to attract in some good stuff rather than get beaten down with morbid filters of news stories.

Method

01. As much as you can, remove the following toxic aspects from your life:

- News stories (often negative to capture mass attention)
- Toxic friends who "bring you down"
- Negative images (thrillers, horror movies, news pictures of terror)
- Processed foods, meat, caffeine, frozen foods, aerosol sprays
- Gossip
- Trading "poor me" stories
- Feeling poor and focusing on lack
- Clutter and mess
- Telling or hearing untruths

Notes:
....
....
....

02. Replace the toxic aspects with the following to aid harmony:

- Uplifting music, books, ideas, visuals, and stories

- Happy friends who make you laugh and are happy themselves

- Being around nature and natural water

- Fresh food—lots of fruit and vegetables, vitamins and minerals

- Physical exercise

- Meditation, quiet time, daily reflection, gratitude journal writing, goal setting

- Cleanliness, integrity, honesty

- Anything that brings you into alignment with love—cooking, music, singing, dancing, walking your dog, loving your partner, taking a relaxing bath, having a massage, watching the sun rise, hopscotch, looking at a rose as if it's for the first time

- Being appreciative for everything there is in this life

Outcome

Just by brushing up your life with the elimination of a few toxic aspects and introducing some high-end vibrancy enhancers, you will change your circumstances radically. Try it today.

Tool 12: The boomerang effect

Whatever you would like more of in your life (e.g. money, love, joy, kindness) begin by giving away some of this very thing you desire. For example, if you are looking for love, then begin by upgrading the love aspect in your life. Love yourself more; really ramp up the love you have for yourself and allow yourself some positive focus and adoration and kind inner mind chat. Give out love to others through words and actions to those in your everyday life and even to complete strangers. You will then see more love showing up in your own life.

How does this work? Through the act of giving something to others (love, money, or support for example), you are sending clear signals to your mind machine that you already have plenty of this in your life—so much in fact that you can happily give it away. You are vibrating to this tune, and through the Law of Attraction, you will then be bringing more of the same through your vibration-attracting power.

Notes:

....

....

....

Tool 13: Prosperity pipeline

Method

01. Create a new feeling about whatever it is that you want more of in your life and feel that you already have this in abundance.

02. Make a point of giving out whatever it is you want more of freely to others with an open heart and with grace. Do not do so in order to receive.

03. As you give, notice the true joy activated in your heart.

Outcome

Through the like-attracts-like principle, you will notice that what you are giving away and therefore focusing on, will come back to you like a boomerang. By creating a space with giving, we leave room for more of the same to flow into our lives.

Flow is a key to prosperity.

Tool 13: Prosperity pipeline

This exercise is an excellent way of opening up your prosperity stream.

It can also be used as a releasing exercise when there is something that you would like to get rid of deep inside yourself.

Method

01. First, go inside and take notice of the infinite aspect of nature. Notice how you are operating in a rhythm and are completely connected to the universe. Notice that the universe is infinitely abundant and works rhythmically, in tune with the cycles of seasons, tides, night and day, and so on. We are all connected to nature in a profound way. Feel a sense of "I am nature and nature is everything."

Get deeply into the idea that you are part of the universe and intertwined with this rhythm that operates within the whole system. We are all part of the ebb and flow of life. We are simply witnesses to its ups and downs, ins and outs, highs and lows. Just notice this and sense the rhythmic beat of life both within and outside.

02. Close your eyes, go deeper inside yourself, and tune into your heartbeat.

03. Imagine a large pipeline and locate it connecting to either your heart or your solar plexus (just above your rib cage in the center of your body, at the front), whichever feels most appropriate for you. There is no right or wrong way to do this, as long as it's clear in your mind's eye.

Notes:

....

....

....

04. Now imagine that you are breathing in and out through this pipeline. As you inhale, picture yourself inhaling all of the abundance and infinite goodness of the universe easily and smoothly. As you exhale, allow all toxicity, bad feelings, and negativity to release out and move along the pipe and then get sent up to the clouds easily and safely. Keep doing this for five minutes. As you do so, really imagine the good stuff coming in and the bad stuff going out easily and effortlessly.

Outcome

Do this twice a day for a week and you will notice an increase in vitality, abundance, and feeling richer. You will also notice a feeling of expansive well-being floating through you and a wonderful release of toxic memories, anxieties, and stresses floating out.

Tool 14: Access all areas

You are a body; you are an energy source; you are who you are; you are everything that is in the universe; you are a cosmic mind; you are full of potential; you are a genius; you are capable of anything; you are conscious; part of you is unconscious and you have an Access All Areas pass to all that is.

I used to love working on big production music shows such as the MTV Europe Music Awards or Michael Jackson's live shows at Radio City in New York. By being a big shot on the production side of things, you could get the most precious of all passes: Access All Areas. You had arrived if you were given one of these.

Straight into Madonna's dressing room, pop in to say hello to George Michael, hang out with Michael Hutchence at the bar, ask Bono if he wants a hand with anything, tell Bowie he needs to move fast and get on stage please, and sit with Michael Jackson as he asks if you can get him booked onto the next Orient Express train out of town to visit Europe, for him and his monkeys, and offers to have you join him for the ride. All of these things and more happened to me with an AAA pass.

You have an AAA pass too, but one that is much better than this. Your AAA pass, your subconscious, will allow you access to all wisdom and to every potentiality that has ever been or ever will be, direct into the universal mind. With this access comes the potential to create anything, absolutely anything, and

Notes:
....
....
....

download whatever you want, on immediate call, every time. If you use your subconscious well, you have access to this gateway and a bridge to a world of infinite wonder.

By connecting with your higher self, you can connect to your own AAA pass. This can be done with very little effort through gentle mindfulness.

Method
01. Go into some reflection time. This can be done by going for a walk in nature, relaxing on a beach, lying still under a tree, sitting quietly and reading a passage from a book, and just being in the moment. There is an inner bridge we can imagine going across and into a deep sense of peace, relaxation, and quietness.

02. Whatever activity or non-activity you choose, practice feeling "being in the moment of now" and just allow yourself to enjoy being yourself. It's a simple, rejuvenating, and powerful process.

Outcome
By regular connection, you get solutions provided quickly and easily to life issues. Your subconscious is brought into the mix, which has a far greater solving power than your conscious mind. Problems quickly fall away and solutions will appear as if by magic.

Tool 15: Show me the money

I love seeing money all over the place. As I open a drawer, there is cash. As I open my purse, there are always dollars in abundance. As I open up my desk, I find it full of bills. I keep purses in all of my bags with some money in them. In my chest of drawers, I have numerous envelopes dotted around each containing wads of cash.

Cash is everywhere in my life. How do you think this makes me feel?

Rich, that's what.

Method
01. When you get paid, take out a chunk of cash that you feel comfortable with. It may be $10 or $100 or $500. It doesn't matter.

02. Make sure that you take this cash and liberally sprinkle it (safely) in attractive envelopes or purses all over your home, car, and desk. Be sure to put this cash in places that belong to you and where you are likely to see it every day.

Notes:
....
....
....

Outcome

To see money everywhere you go is a great device for feeling rich—in your car, in your home, in your office, in your bag, as you open a drawer. It is a constant reminder to you that you have plenty of money and that this money is everywhere.

This will build the feeling that you have a wonderful abundance of cash and richness. It also means that you always have a plentiful supply of cash around and never have the feeling of running out. I top off my cash supplies each month and do the sprinkling around regularly.

It's a good feeling and always makes me feel rich and abundant while doing it.

Tool 16: Laugh your head off

Laughing is one of the best medicines around to make you feel good and to increase your vibrancy and frequency. You cannot laugh and feel depressed. You cannot laugh and be down. You cannot laugh without raising your vibrancy and your magnetism for goodness.

We all need to laugh more. When I ran Paul McKenna's personal development business with him, we laughed a lot and had laughing sessions beginning at the start of each day. It worked wonders and kept us performing our best. Paul and I would spend the majority of our day, every day, laughing our heads off and telling jokes. We couldn't stop; it was part of the fabric of the day.

Was it just coincidence that we became more and more successful each day? No. We were laughing so much we couldn't fail.

Method

01. Go to a comedy show, watch a funny movie, find your funniest friend and hang out together.

02. Laugh your head off.

03. Keep doing this every day of your life.

Outcome

If you laugh a lot every day, your vibration will keep rising.

With this frequency change, there will be an increase in your attraction of success, harmony, and happiness.

There is nothing better than laughing your way to success.

Notes:
....
....
....

Happiness ...

Tool 17.
What makes you happy?
Think about it ...

....
....
....
....
....
....
....
....
....
....
....
....
....
....
....
....
....
....
....
....

Outcome

By engaging regularly in the activities that make us happy, we build on feelings of well-being and happiness. We are meant to be living in joy and happiness—this is the reason for our being. Often, we are running in the fast lane so hard that life has become one long list of To Do's. Instead, run a long list of To Be's. **Start with being happy.**

Tool 17: This makes me happy

Tool 17: This makes me happy

Now this one may sound too simple to be powerful, but stay with me for a moment.

Do you know what makes you truly happy in life? Write down a list of exactly what makes you happy.

It may be being with your love, spending time with your kids, hiking, playing sport, walking your dog, having dinner with friends, travellng, reading, watching a movie, line dancing or train spotting, for example.

Method
01. Make a list here and be as adventurous and wild with this list as you can.

→

Notes:

....
....
....
....
....
....
....
....
....
....
....
....

Things that make me happy:

01. ....
02. ....
03. ....
04. ....
05. ....
06. ....
07. ....
08. ....
09. ....
10. ....
11. ....
12. ....
13. ....
14. ....
15. ....
16. ....
17. ....
18. ....
19. ....
20. ....

02. Now, consider how many of these things you make a point of doing regularly.

Aim to do all of these things at least once in the coming week/s.

Make a point of planning as many things from your happy list as you can. Make a start with at least 2 of these today.

Tool 18: Design your own avatar

When we shift our alignments of who we are being, our life experiences change. Many of us build our own avatars of ourselves online–chosen representations of who we are being. Here you simply transfer this concept into life. You choose a new avatar of yourself, step into this, and come from this place.

> **Av·a·tar** noun
> *A computer user's representation of themselves or the alter ego as in computer games.*

Method
01. Breathe in the possibility now that anything is possible, everything is doable, and that you can be/do/have anything you choose in this lifetime. Consider this as true for a moment.

02. Once you have come to the conclusion that you can be/do/have anything, align with the version of yourself that is already doing the having and the being. This is where your creative powers come in. Design and be a new version of you now that has everything you want.

03. Decide to be the person who has these things, act like them, think like them, have the posture, dress like them, and do the same activities as them. Get the feeling of this–create a new you.

Create a new version of you like a new avatar. You can do it. You are transforming and changing every moment into a new being, so positively design your change. Our cells and every part of our bodies change constantly and remake themselves into new versions. Everything about us is in a state of constant renewal. Well, how about doing this with who you are choosing to be?

Who are you choosing to be today? Make it a great and much bigger, better, and more successful you than you would have imagined possible previously. Be it, breathe it, and act from this place of being this new version of you.

Outcome
This is a great technique for quickly sliding into a new version of who you choose to be. It is a quick way to release old patterns and an old profile and bring in a new set of values and intentions.

Notes:
....
....
....

Tool 19: Meditate to manifest

Most successful people I know have learned to somehow tap into the connecting power of the highest creativity.

We can all tap into this. One of the best ways is through meditation.

I learned Transcendental Meditation many years ago and practice it twice daily as a matter of routine. It has helped me become more successful, happier, luckier, and more creative than ever before. I am calmer and find it hard to get stressed by anything these days. Within a week of starting to meditate, my soul mate came into my life unexpectedly after a long wait. He was everything that I wanted and more.

Consider taking a course in meditation in order to access these higher powers for good. This will give you direct access to ideas, wisdom, solutions, creativity, full health, powering rejuvenation, success, luck, fortune, improved memory, stress reduction, calmness, synchronicities, and many other benefits. People find that they get rid of addictions and damaging habits through developing a practice of mindful meditation of some kind. Here's a tool to begin the feelings of getting into a meditative state.

Method

01. Sit down at a time where you will have at least fifteen minutes to yourself. Switch off your phone, take off your shoes, and relax. Sit up straight with your feet flat on the floor, take some deep breaths in, exhale deeply, and close your eyes.

02. Allow your awareness to be placed onto your gentle breath. You don't need to do anything now—you just need to "be." As thoughts come in, watch them go by as an observer. There is no push with this method. You just sit in quietness and experience what it feels like to be "you." As you do this, your body will relax, your cells will relax, you will relax, and a natural regeneration and stress release process will begin.

03. Do nothing now for fifteen minutes except enjoy the time.

Outcome
Connecting and getting to know and feel your higher self will give you immense benefits, including an increase in your wellness, vitality, and feelings of well-being.

Notes:
....
....
....

Meditation is the single most important daily activity you can do. You will create abundance fast, get powered up and in tune with the big picture. It has the potential to completely revolutionize your life in magnificent ways—and always does.

Meditation is one of the great secret tools of a happy and successful life.

Tool 20: Affirmation lists

Affirming our choices and intentions daily powers up a major attraction factor of positive experience into our lives. Establishing a routine of affirming the positive choices you make directs you to success fast.

Method
01. Write out your own affirmations for each of the following categories:

Wealth
Example: I am grateful for having plenty of money and abundance in my life already and to be living knowing that I am always looked after with enough money and plenty of what I need.

....

....

....

....

....

Health
Example: I am grateful to have a healthy body and be increasing in vitality every day with a balance in eating, sleeping, working, and resting.

....

....

....

....

....

....

Happiness
Example: I appreciate and affirm my positive feelings and choose to stay happy and upbeat as my default position.

....

....

....

....

....

Love
Example: I feel so lucky to have plenty of love in my life, moment by moment, day by day. I know what love feels like and I enjoy the feeling.

....

....

....

....

....

Contentment
Example: I feel positively content in my life being who I am and enjoying the journey as perfection unfolds.

....

....

....

....

....

Notes:

....

....

....

Direction
Example: I feel so clear in my own life direction and it feels good to know where I am choosing to go next. I know that I am right on track and in a perfect place on my own journey.

....

....

....

....

....

Fun & Adventure
Example: I love expecting great adventures and I appreciate all of the adventures and fun that I experience along the way each and every day.

....

....

....

....

....

02. Repeat these affirmations ten times daily. It works to write them down, say them out loud, or say them to yourself. Doing all of these things really powers up the effect.

Outcome
By clearly stating our affirmations, we power up our minds to be clear about what we choose to resonate and vibrate with and, therefore, what we are calling in to attract into our lives.

Using affirmations is like filling out the authorized application forms for manifesting with clarity. It works.

Notes:
....

....

....

Part C

Tool 21: No limits

Tool 21: No limits

Imagining a life without limits is the way to go for manifesting greatness in life. The more we imagine what our lives would be like with no restrictions on success or happiness, the more we see them expand.

Method

01. Make a list of the things you would choose to do if you knew there were no limits. It can be anything. Stretch your mind and beliefs and really use your imagination to answer this one. List them here.

Write this list as if you have all the money, time, ability, skills, opportunities, and resources as you need to create your goals.

There are no limitations in life, and all of these things you have written down are possible if you believe they are. Make sure these are positive, relevant to you and your life, and are backed with positive intentions.

02. Next, write down three steps needed to get closer to achieving each of these and then add them to your goals list. The sky is not the limit; our belief systems are the only limitations aspects. If you have beliefs

I choose to create:

01. _____

_____

02. _____

_____

03. _____

_____

04. _____

_____

05. _____

_____

06. _____

_____

07. _____

_____

Notes:

....

....

....

that say these things are not possible, how about revisiting those beliefs and making some changes to make them possible? They are your beliefs; you get to choose what sticks and stays or what gets changed. You can change any belief you want.

So consider that all of these things are possible and start from there. Everything and anything is possible so long as you believe it is.

Outcome

This exercise allows you to think up ideas and goals which go outside of your belief systems and allows you to consider things that you would otherwise view as unattainable.
You can stretch and you can think big while doing this.

It's always good to aim high and out of your comfort zone. That way life becomes exciting and fun.

Steps to get closer:

01. i. _____ ii. _____ iii. _____

02. i. _____ ii. _____ iii. _____

03. i. _____ ii. _____ iii. _____

04. i. _____ ii. _____ iii. _____

05. i. _____ ii. _____ iii. _____

06. i. _____ ii. _____ iii. _____

07. i. _____ ii. _____ iii. _____

Notes:
....
....
....

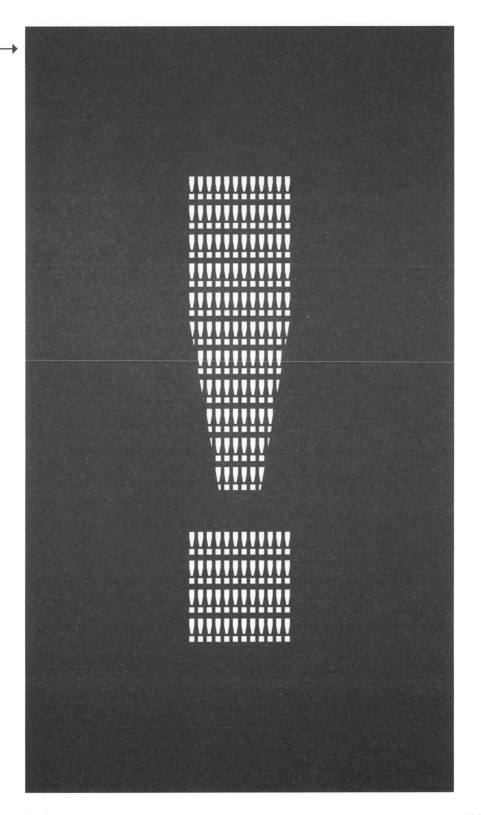

Part C

Tool 22: Last day on earth

If you knew you only had one day left, what would you do? What would you notice? Would you be more present in your life for those few hours? Yes, you would. Try to translate this into an everyday approach to life and make sure that each day really counts. Notice more, criticize less. Appreciate all; celebrate the simple things. Notice the incredible design of a tree, take time to smell the roses, sing a song, say hi to everyone like you care, be present, breathe and notice the smell of the air, hear the birds singing, and marvel at the movement of the sun. Notice it all with love, appreciation, wonder, and thanks. See everything more clearly, smell the perfumes of life, touch the sensuality of nature, and feel the feelings that accompany the journey that is your day.

Method

01. Live like it's your last day, with mindfulness, appreciation, and joy. Notice the rhythm of your day— the ebbs and flow of your energy patterns as the hours progress—and make them work for you. Plan your day to correspond with your natural rhythms. Notice when to work, when to relax, when to eat, and when to exercise and try and build your day around the patterns which work best for you. How we spend each day translates to how we end up spending our lives, so build a wonderful routine which includes happy activities in abundance.

Outcome

When you live life with full awareness then you can enjoy the moment of now with extra pleasure. Being "in the now" brings with it a sense of your own happiness, contentment, and fullness of life. It creates a state of supreme appreciation and helps you to focus on the value of all that is. This in turn will increase your manifesting abilities and will bring even more riches and abundance straight to you.

Sometimes life lives us. We should live life.

Today I appreciate:

_____

_____

_____

_____

Notes:

....

....

....

Tool 23: Abundance checklist (see page 189)

This is a great way to plan what you would like, see what you do well, notice the gaps, and improve your lifestyle easily and accurately.

Method
01. Each day, give yourself a mark out of ten for how you are doing with each item. Notice at the end of the week which areas you need to spend more time on to get your life in balance and working in the way you want.

Do this for four weeks and see how you are doing across all of these areas. Keep a file of your charts so you can review your progress. Simply focusing on these sections will bring you more into balance and harmony.

By taking the time to get really honest with yourself about what's happening in each of these life areas and noticing where you can do better, you will be able to access great information on where to make changes and adjustments.

Once you have a sense of where you need to go, you can get there much faster.

Outcome
This will bring more happiness, health, wealth, direction, fun, and positive attraction into your life fast.

Tool 24: Activate your wealth pulse

When you get in the flow or rhythm, then you get in abundance, just as night follows day.

We have all experienced being "in the flow." Sometimes it can take a while to get "in the flow" or in the zone, but once in we know we are good to go. We can keep on track and successfully complete the tasks in front of us. We see the rhythmic patterns of life everywhere: day and night, how spring follows winter, and how waves come in and out on the shore. When we tune in to the rhythm of life and move with it and breathe with it, we harness the technique of allowing full abundance and wealth into our experience. Money flow is an aspect in the rhythmic nature of life. It is an aspect of cosmic energy rhythm. Flow with nature and you can easily slip into flow with money and wealth.

Method
Memorize these steps so that you

Notes:

....
....
....

can go through them in sequence without stopping to look at your notes. Blend each step together without pausing.

01. Start by tuning in to rhythms around you. Notice rhythm at work in the space where you are right now. If you are outdoors, feel the breeze, hear wings flutter, or tune into the harmony of birds singing. Inside, tune to the ticking of a clock, the hum of your PC, the dripping of a faucet, or whatever repeating noise is present. Listen at a subtle, natural level.

02. Spend ten minutes observing closely, repeating actions and sounds—breath, heartbeat, walking, jogging, birds singing, waves, the clock, day changes, coastal tides, etc. It may be that you begin to notice your own internal rhythms as well—something that we have learned to block out most of the time and rarely notice (until something goes wrong). Some people have never tuned in to their own rhythms inside: sensing their own heartbeats, blinking eyes, breathing through their nostrils, the subtle noises in the ears, or inner pulsating sensations.

03. In a quiet place where you will not be disturbed, close your eyes and connect with your breath. Breathe in and out continuously and smoothly without pause (no space between the breaths) for ten minutes. Allow your breathing to rise and fall, like a wheel with its own momentum. As thoughts come up, just let them drift by. Keep your awareness on this connected breathing.

04. Return to breathing normally and move your attention to your heart. Notice a pulse in the heart region that is not your heartbeat. When you notice a pulsation that is in the heart region but that is not from the heart, allow your attention to settle on this pulse (this is your wealth pulse). As thoughts come up, just let them glide away while paying most attention to the pulse. Keep doing this for ten minutes. You may or may not notice this pulse the first time. Don't worry if you can't find it first time around; just try again another time and you will get it.

05. Regardless of whether you found the pulse above or not, now look for a more physical wealth rhythm. It involves a sense of rhythmic movement in your body; it may be that your head moves gently from side to side, your body shakes gently or strongly, your eyelids flutter, or you

Notes:

....

....

....

might experience involuntary face movements; people have different responses and there is no right or wrong. Just notice your own physical response. Do this for a further ten minutes.

06. Lie down and rest for ten minutes. This is necessary and allows your systems to come back into alignment again. Come back out slowly, just as you would from a meditation.

07. Make notes about what you found.

Outcome

This exercise tunes you directly into your wealth consciousness and rhythm. It will activate a movement and a flow in of money and all aspects of wealth.

In short, you will become wealthier through your increased focus and awareness of flow and your own internal money rhythm. Make it a once (or better twice) daily practice to visit your wealth pulse and money rhythm, preferably at the start or end of the day.

Finding my wealth pulse I noticed:

Finding my physical money rhythm I noticed:

Fast tips for increasing abundance

If you want to get wealthy, hang out with rich people

We are our environments. We are what we eat, what we think, what we feel. We quickly become who we hang out with. One of the fastest ways to get the wealth attraction factor is to make a point of hanging out with rich people in a wealthy environment.

Be in a clean smart environment for happiness and success

In order to have happiness, calm, contentedness, peacefulness, and success, you must have an environment that is clean, uncluttered, and beautiful—one which represents who you are choosing to be.

Do some decluttering and retuning and beautifying of your environment and space today.

Clothes show

Choose clothes and an image that matches who you are choosing to be. These are your external signals about the kind of person you are vibrating as and being. Clothes and appearance are important as a signal device to transmit important information about who you are.

People wearing a suit or jeans, a uniform, sweats, or a wedding dress are all making very different and powerful nonverbal statements about their vibrational choices and state of being that day. We pick up and collect a lot of information through our visual senses.

How we dress and hold ourselves tells others a great deal about us. It will affect the quality and nature of our interactions with others.

Notes:

....

....

....

Magnet swallowing

Imagine that you have swallowed a powerful magnet. This magnet has unique properties. It is the most powerful magnet known to man. However, this one does not attract metal. It attracts only everything that you are wishing for and choosing to bring into your life.

Imagine your inner positive magnet and say:

"I have activated you to attract everything I wish for and more. All for the greatest good. Thank you. It's already done. Show me."

As you go through your day, imagine your inner magnet doing its work.

Bless your food

Years ago, as children, many of us were taught to say grace at the table before eating and after a meal. The Law of Attraction shows us that blessing (giving love to) anything will raise the frequency of ourselves and whatever we are blessing, because of the powerful focus of the blessing.

To bless our food, give thanks, and raise the frequency of what we are about to put inside ourselves makes a powerful difference to our frequencies and transmission. Build more blessings and grace into your day today.

This is a great way to power up the love and appreciation aspects in our day and in our bodies.

Feel, be, attract.

Notes:

....

....

....

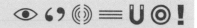

Tool 25: Create a master mind group

This is a great technique to bring success to any project.

Method

Bring together a group of great minds who are able to work in harmony together, with a clear set of intentions, and you will be creating a massive mind-power battery pack to energize and bring success in faster.

Add some energy of enthusiasm and excitement to the group and then set to work knowing that you have a proven formula for success by establishing the power of a master mind group.

> "No two minds ever come together without creating a third, invisible, intangible force which may be likened to a third mind."
> Napoleon Hill
> *Think and Grow Rich* (1937)

Outcome

This master mind strategy is a powerful formula used by many successful leaders. Incredible mind power is created by this joining up of two or more minds.

It usually delivers way above expectations in support of the stated intentions.

> By creating a group of minds with a harmonized focus on a determined goal, the power of manifesting is set to work.
>
> Consider this to be your secret weapon for success.

Burning desire + Clear intention + Focus + Faith + Gratitude = **A master mind team**

To sum up . . .

The tools provided within this chapter give us the opportunity to create a life of infinite potential, enthusiasm, abundance, health, wealth, and, most worthy of all, happiness.

Let's use them and do it.

You have the key to a magnificent life and infinite power through the taming and understanding of the power of your own mind.

Notes:

....

....

....

Next

So what's next?
Life gets better
right now.

A. So what's next?

Together we have gone through the rules and the tools for creating your own reality.

Through reading this book and listening to the audios you now understand how it works, how to do it, and have a tool kit of practical ways to boost your happiness and success.

Not only have you read how it works —you have had it downloaded direct into your neurology.

This sets you up as powerful and ready to go, with new strategies for approaching life having been already preinstalled.

Have you been having fun with this along the way?

Notes:

....

....

....

> # Your life is going to be as good as you can imagine.

Does the excitement about what's possible start to build now? Yes.

Does life start to get really interesting from here? Yes.

Life starts to gets better and better. We build improved life experiences day by day through getting more mindful about what we are thinking and feeling each moment.

B. We create our world

Through the chapters, you have learned about how creating reality works. We have been through the concept that we live in an attraction-based universe and seen how to make this work for your own happiness and success.

We now begin to understand more deeply that we create everything that shows up in our lives.

The exciting news is that by knowing this you can do a much better job of positively creating your experience. Through new ways of being, you can create a much better life by design. You are able to do it more consciously, more accurately, more positively, and more expansively than ever before. If you can think it, it is possible to create it.

Your life is about to become a whole lot better when you start using these tools daily.

> You can expect more happiness, more joy, more inspiration, more love, more abundance, more wealth, more opportunities, more wisdom, more satisfaction, more contentment, and more focus and direction by following these instructions. **Is that OK with you?**

We have covered a lot of ground here on reality creation with how it works, how to do it, and the tool box of practical tools.

Now you are ready to step forward and start implementing and using this in your life—every day, moment by moment. The more you become aware of what you're thinking, feeling, imagining, and saying, the more you can direct the style of your life.

This manual is a way of life and a lifestyle, not a one-off exercise.

The instructions contained within this book provide you with a tool kit to live life with gusto. Your life can expand into whatever you choose. If you were to ask, "Do you really believe we can all do, be, and have anything

Notes:
....
....
....

we choose?" I would say, "Yes, 100%. And the findings of quantum science show us that this is true."

You can find out for yourself by test driving the method and seeing how your life expands and transforms.

There are so many incredible stories of how people's lives have changed for the better by following these techniques—new soul mates, better jobs, more money, health, and increased optimism have all come from using these instructions and tools.

Many people say to me that they love the positive outlook and perspective that this work brings them. It is true that many people begin living with a sense of freedom and joy perhaps for the first time in their lives once they start applying these tools.

Good things that are already happening:

_____

_____

_____

_____

_____

_____

_____

_____

_____

_____

_____

_____

_____

_____

_____

_____

Part C

C. Your onward journey starts now

Begin your own journey exploring new ways of living now. Begin noticing the synchronicities that will start coming through, the chance meetings with new people with the right connections, serendipitous moments appearing more frequently, and doors of opportunity flying open. All of these things will happen more when you start this process. Watch for them and expect them.

When people begin on this journey with focus, they remark on how quickly the things they have wanted to create for a long time begin to arrive. It's like the barriers come down, the resistance releases, the unhelpful blockers fly away, and a better life appears to unfold and arrives faster than they could have imagined possible.

Remember this method works 100% of the time when used precisely. This is because reality is based around laws of the universe that never fail. These principles are in operation and at work all of the time.

It makes no difference how clever you are, what job you have, how influential your friends are, or how much money you have right now. The process doesn't discriminate in this way. You can create whatever you wish for by following this procedure, regardless of where you are today.

Begin somewhere. Take a few steps. Start doing the exercises and keep doing them. Start telling a different story—and begin to notice the changes.

D. Life is transforming already

When people begin on this journey of new ways of thinking about life, it is common for them to have phone calls coming in out of the blue about new opportunities they have imagined, relationships all around start to change and improve, money begins to appear from unexpected avenues, and so on.

We begin to see that the right things come in at the right time. You may find that friends fall away and change. When you change your energy and viewpoint, then things change both on the inside and on the outside. It's all for good.

E. Fully loaded and fully responsible

We can no longer issue blame to others about what goes on in our

Notes:

....

....

....

lives. With this new approach, we begin to see that everything comes from our own inner mind activity and begins with how we are conducting our inner world of thoughts and feelings. This inner activity always creates what shows up in our outer world.

It's like going to a mind-gym daily: the more you practice these techniques, the stronger your manifesting muscles become and the better you get.

The more you work with these tools, the more successful you will become. It works this way.

F. Happiness breeds success

Have you noticed that the really successful people tend to be upbeat and positive with a go-getting style? When they get pushed down, they rise up again like loaded spring coils. Did they get like this because of their success? No. They were already using this approach of keeping their feelings buoyant in order to get their success in the first place.

You can only be successful when you keep good feelings flowing inside. This is the nature of how success works. When you learn to bounce back and feel good whatever gets in your way, then you are already well on your path to a successful life.

Many of the followers of this work are already very successful in their own fields—screenwriters, directors, TV producers, artists, singers, musicians, entrepreneurs, stock traders, teachers, doctors—they come to explore how to get more successful and strengthen their inner-techniques of running their successful lives. They already intuitively know that their success comes from within and they want to power this up further.

So where does happiness and success come from? You know this already. It comes from the inside out.

How well we run our minds determines how successful our lives become and how happy we are.

We can decide to be happy instantly.

Now is a good time to decide to be happy.

When people begin to do this, large smiles tend to cross their faces as they get a whiff of this truth: **anything and everything is possible**.

Notes:
....
....
....

The biggest rule of all is that we create everything 100% with our minds.

> **Instruction:**
>
> Choose to be happy now.
> Go directly there. And stay there.*
>
> * Note to self: follow this instruction to the letter.

We are here for a short time. Let's give it our best shot using everything we know. Go for the high life. Aim high.

The instructions in this book are derived from a melting pot of ancient wisdom and modern science and are designed to bring you directly into happiness and success regardless of where you are right now.

So get good at this. Practice it. Tell your friends. Spread the news about how it works. The better we get at it, the more we can all live happily and successfully together.

- Have more fun to get happy and successful

- Get involved with life

- Listen up

- Live listening to your heart

- Go for it

- Get going with life

- Notice what you think and feel

- Move on up with your emotions

- Love living in happiness and success

G. We are part of nature
Nature is abundant and infinite. We are part of human nature.

We only need to look at the sky, the sea, the seasons, the grass growing, leaves on the trees, the multitude of species, fauna and flora, animals and insects, birds, and all wildlife in its greatest wildness to see that nature is abundant, infinite, and awesome. And so are we.

We are part of nature's flow. By harnessing the power of nature, we can be, do, and have anything we choose. We can learn to be in flow like the seasons. We can learn to guide our thoughts, emotions, and feelings in the knowledge that, by doing this, we are consciously setting our life direction and creating our personal story.

We know how to make it work successfully. We now have the

Notes:
....
....
....

> **There is only now.**

operating manual. Many of us have spent years reacting to and being commentators on how things already are in our lives.

To make the switch to realize that we are the ongoing creators and have full power to control our experience through how we think, feel, and experience is quite a tall order. It takes strength to do it, but we can and it's easy to do once you get rolling with it.

The methods, ideas, and principles in this book give hope and optimism for everyone.

It means that we can take stock, take charge, and make some positive changes for good. If we fail, we can come up with a thousand excuses, but there are no good reasons.

H. We can do anything

We can reduce what we do by 50%, increase our fun by 50%, and see our success soar infinitely as a result. The power is in the thinking, feeling, and believing—not the action. By increasing our fun in life, we increase our success. Life is meant to be fun; this is the natural order of what we are designed to be.

We are happy beings, yet many of us have forgotten about the well-being platform we've come from.

For better results, we can radically change the way that we operate by moving away from examining how life is and instead viewing it through a filter of how we choose it to be.

We set out our desires, create the feelings of already having what we choose in our lives, and use our emotions to guide us, moving ever closer to happiness and joy in order to create the lives of our dreams.

Is this truly possible? Yes. By becoming mindful of our thoughts and emotions and using the patterns described here, we can move into joy.

Life is now—not later. It isn't when we meet our soul mate, get a job, make enough money, buy a house, get married, or become parents. It is none of these things. **Life is now.**

The speed of technology and change has never been so dramatic. The children of our generation are well set to navigate this speed and changes and they already use new technology brilliantly in their fresh, young lives

Notes:

....

....

....

with excitement and a thrilling sense of wonder.

Children will be great users of this information. They already operate in the now; they already know how to have fun; they already play all the time; they are magnificent joy machines; they laugh; they imagine and pretend to be so many fun things; they understand about having a lightness of being; they know how to heal fast; they forgive and move on; they don't dwell on yesterday's stuff; they are vibrating love and are full of joy and happiness when in their default position. Children and animals have so much to show us about being magnificent.

We are not here to be observers of the success of others or as gatherers of material possessions. No, we are here on a mission to experience joy.

That's it.

We only need to "ask, allow, and receive" and it will be delivered simply, on time, and guaranteed.

I. Are you ready for change in your life now?
Of course you are. Whatever is going on in your life, this will be a time that you can look back and give thanks for what is happening now. Whatever you have running in your life, be sure that it's leading you directly toward the path that you need at this moment, to tune up to your life's perfection.

Everything we learn and experience is valuable and teaches us important lessons. We have created and manifested where we are now for good reasons.

The fact that you have found this book at this point in your life means that you are ready for the information given here and can use it meaningfully now.

J. Reach for your desires
Remember that fears and a troubled mind are your worst enemies and will take you directly to the place where you don't want to be, so pivot and put your attention toward what you choose to create and magnify into your experience.

We have the tools here for living life in love, abundance, and success. We are the creators of it all and are now ready to take some new steps, armed with these laws and principles. The laws are ancient, yet the understanding is new.

Notes:

....

....

....

Let's make it amazing.

This information has only become available to all of us in recent times and was previously rarely known about outside of well-guarded secret societies. It's powerful information.

Encouraging one another, helping our children to learn these principles, and bringing in mind-discipline will enable us to bring happiness and success into our daily living.

With significant and fast changes happening in our world today, we need to find harmony and better living fast.

This begins inside, with upgrading our internal mind software.

The tools described in this book are here for you to do this. If you are reading this now, then you are already on your way to great changes.

We are born free and happy. To live life with a sense of freedom and happiness is the way to successful living. We start today.

By moving our minds and emotions into those good feeling places, we can do anything.

What's next?